THE STORY OF TILFORD

From prehistoric times to 2000 A.D.

A short history of a Surrey Village and its people

Captain John E Franklin BSc(Eng) DIC RN

*A millennium project commissioned by Tilford Parish Council
December 2000*

Copyright © John F. Franklin,
Wey Cottage, Squires Hill Lane, Tilford
Surrey GU10 2AD.

Published by Tilford Parish Council.
December 2000.

The moral right of John Franklin to be identified as the author of this work has been asserted in accordance with the Copyright, Designs and Patents Act of 1988.

This book is sold subject to the condition that it shall not be lent, resold, hired out, or otherwise circulated without the copyright holder's prior consent. No part may be reproduced, stored in a retrieval system, or transmitted, in any form or by any means, electronic, mechanical, photocopying, recording, or otherwise, without the prior permission of the copyright holder.

ISBN © 09539644-0-X

Printed by Blackdown Press Limited
Fernhurst, Haslemere, Surrey GU27 3EE

Front Cover. View of Tilford Green in the late 19th Century. From an original watercolour by Doug Pelling of Tilford. The blacksmith's shop, demolished after World War II, can be seen in front of The Barley Mow P.H. and Tilford Green Cottages.

Preface

Over the last three years, I have been writing short articles about Tilford which have been published in the parish magazine. It was suggested to me that I could draw on the research I had done for these articles and put together a short history of the village. Commissioned by Tilford Parish Council to commemorate the millennium, the present book is the result. The work involved has led me to many different sources of information. I have had much assistance from very many people and would like to take this opportunity of acknowledging their help and thanking them for their patience and goodwill.

It would be impossible for me to name everyone who has come to my aid but in particular I should like to thank Mary Mackey for her advice and help in tracing documents at the Surrey History Centre; Chris Hellier, Jean Parratt and Peggy Parks at the Farnham Museum for answering my many queries and offering me their encouragement; the late Philip Brooks for his advice on the Winchester archives; the staff of the Hampshire Record Office for their guidance and help over the Bishop of Winchester's records; and Alexa Barrow for her support at the Rural Life Centre and for first suggesting the project. Dr David Bird, Principal Archaeologist of Surrey County Council, Pat Heather, and Alexa Barrow generously gave of their time to read relevant chapters of the book, and their advice and suggestions have been invaluable. I was able to draw on the booklet *Tilford through the Ages*, which covers much of Tilford's history and was pleased to receive advice from Graham Collyer and Barbara Gregory, contributors to that publication. Doug Pelling very generously agreed to paint an original watercolour for the front cover of the book which enhances it enormously, and for which I thank him most warmly. Many other people in Tilford gave me the benefit of their personal reminiscences and archival photographs, and for these I am particularly grateful. Members of Tilford Parish Council have been most supportive and encouraging and to them and to the many other local individuals and organisations who have assisted in the book's production, I offer my warmest thanks.

The written records of a small village such as Tilford are at best far from complete and sometimes frustratingly absent. In many instances, and particularly in the early periods where facts and figures are hard to come by, I have been led to conclusions based on flimsy evidence; in other cases, I have had to make guesses which fit the sparse facts available but are unsupported by any direct evidence. Inevitably, there will be errors but I hope these will be sufficiently few in number not to mar the integrity of the overall story.

John E Franklin
Tilford
December 2000

IV

THE STORY OF TILFORD

CONTENTS

	Page
Preface	*iii*
List of Illustrations	*vii*
Introduction	*ix*
Chapter 1: Facts and Figures	*1*
Chapter 2: Landscape and Land	*8*
Chapter 3: Prehistoric Tilford	*11*
Chapter 4: The Roman Occupation	*18*
Chapter 5: The Dark Ages	*24*
Chapter 6: The Coming of the Normans	*32*
Chapter 7: Mediaeval Tilford	*41*
Chapter 8: Tudor Times	*52*
Chapter 9: The Civil War and its Aftermath	*62*
Chapter 10: The Landed Gentry	*69*
Chapter 11: Paternalism and Change	*83*
Chapter 12: Progress and Plenty	*110*
Glossary	*136*
Further Reading	*140*
Index	*145*

The author and publishers are grateful to the copyright holders for permission to reproduce the following illustrations:

The Ahmadiyya Muslim Association U.K.: 64.
Mrs Susan Allison, Mrs Winifred Harper-Smith, & Mrs Amy Hall: 56.
British Geological Survey: 5.
The British Library: 12.
Mrs Estelle M. Carter: 61.
The Curator, Lords Cricket Ground: 47.
Mr Geoff. Dye: 49
English Heritage: 18.
Miss Anthea How: 39.
Harry Margary Maps: 2.
The Museum of Farnham: 42, 43.
The Old Kiln Museum Trust: frontispiece, 33, 41, 44, 46, 48, 57, 58, 63.
Mr Douglas A. Pelling: front cover.
Phillimore & Co. Ltd: 15.
The Public Record Office: 26.
The late Mr Martin C. De Roemer: 10.
F. Sturt Ltd: 37.
Surrey Archaeological Society: 7, 11, 22.
Surrey History Service: 27, 28, 30, 31, 32, 34, 38, 55, 60.
Thomas Family Archives: 40, 45, 53, 62.
Tilford Parish Council: 35, 51.
Tilford Women's Institute: 54.

Frontispiece: View of Tilford Green in the 1860's (reproduced from the Ware family album 31.22 by kind permission of the Old Kiln Museum Trust, Tilford.)

List of Illustrations

		Page
-	*View of Tilford Green in the 1860's*	Frontispiece
1.	The Location of Tilford in Surrey	1
2.	Part of Map of Surrey by John Norden 1594	2
3.	Tilford Parish Boundaries	4
4.	The Population of Tilford	6
5.	The Shores of the Wealden Lake 100 million years ago	8
6.	Change in the Course of the River Wey over the last two million years	10
7.	Mesolithic Tranchet Axes from the Edge Collection	13
8.	Prehistoric Remains in Tilford	15
9.	Roman Remains in Tilford	19
10.	A Roman Jar from 'Overwey' in Tilford	20
11.	Egyptian 'Ushabti'	22
12.	Caedwalla's Charter A.D. 688	25
13.	The Bounds of Farnham Manor	27
14.	Postulated Site of the 'Battle of Farnham' A.D. 893	29
15.	Extract from the Surrey Domesday Survey A.D. 1086	33
16.	Line of William the Conqueror's March in 1066	35
17.	The Lands of Waverley Abbey	36
18.	Depiction of Waverley Abbey in the 14th Century	38
19.	Tilford's East Bridge	40
20.	Tilford's Bond Lands	45
21.	Farnham Hundred and its Tithings	47
22.	Portrait of Fitzwilliam, Earl of Southampton	53
23.	Linches (Upper Street) Farmhouse, Tilford	55
24.	Bridgeland (Malthouse) Farmhouse,	61
25.	Bridge House (Bridge Farm), Tilford	63
26.	Hearth Tax Record for Tilford Tithing A.D. 1669/70	67
27.	Tilford House 1854	71
28.	Portrait of Reverend Thomas Tayler (1735-1831)	73
29.	Tilford House Chapel	74
30.	Part of the Map of Elizabeth Abney's Estate in Tilford 1767	75

31.	Portrait of Anne Tayler (1792-1859)	76
32.	Tilford House c. 1905	84
33.	Chapel Farmhouse and Chapel by the Green	85
34.	Portrait of James Ware (1817-1902)	88
35.	Part of 1840 Tithe Map of Tilford	89
36.	Farnham Coach Timetable 1837	90
37.	The Red Rover Coach	91
38.	The Plank Bridge at Sheephatch	92
39.	Henry and Kate Salt at South Bank (Gorse) Cottage	95
40.	Domestic Staff at 'The Barrows' c.1900	96
41.	Harvesting Scene 1850's	98
42.	Fire Practice on Tilford Green c.1897	99
43.	Waverley Abbey Mill c.1890	100
44.	All Saints' School Tilford c.1870	101
45.	All Saints' Church and Parsonage c.1880	102
46.	Tilford's First Village School Tilford in the 1850's	103
47.	William 'Silver Billy' Beldham aged 84	104
48.	Tilford's Drum and Fife Band c.1900	106
49.	The 'Barley Mow' at Tilford c.1900	107
50.	Tilford Institute	108
51.	Notice of the First Parish Meeting at Tilford 4th December 1894	109
52.	Tilford Green and Surroundings	110
53.	Planting the Queen Victoria Diamond Jubilee Oak Tree, 1897	111
54.	Tilford Oak and Oak Cottage c.1860	112
55.	Planting the George V Coronation Oak Tree, 1911	113
56.	Mr. Willie Tilbury and Tilford's Petrol Pump c.1925	115
57.	Troops at Tilford c.1910	116
58.	Waverley Abbey Hospital Ward in World War I	119
59.	Tilford's War Memorial	120
60.	Drawing of Canon Martin Stewart Ware (1871-1934)	122
61.	The Hunt sets off from Tilford Green c.1950	124
62.	Tilford Horticultural Society Committee 1930's	125
63.	Home Guard No 3 Platoon 1944	128
64.	Islamabad	133
65.	The 'Barley Mow' and Cricket on Tilford Green	134

Introduction

Tilford is a village with a long and interesting history. There is evidence of man in Tilford from as far back as Palaeolithic times and it has been a settlement of one sort or another since the Mesolithic Age. Remains from the later Bronze and Iron ages have been identified and in Roman times Tilford was the location of a pottery industry. Possibly from this period but certainly from the time of the Anglo-Saxons, there was a permanent agricultural settlement in which the land was parcelled out in well-regulated and defined areas and allotted to specific settlers and their families. Remarkably, this pattern survived intact right the way through to modern times; it continues to dictate the boundaries of the village and its fields today.

The story of Tilford is the history of an agricultural community, at times moderately prosperous and at other times barely surviving. For many centuries it was virtually cut off from the outside world. Kings and queens have come and gone on the national stage without disturbing its tranquillity. A much more important person in the villagers' lives was the Bishop of Winchester in whose manor of Farnham Tilford lay. The foundation nearby of the great Cistercian Abbey of Waverley in 1128 cast a benign shadow on the village, whilst the Black Death which invaded England in 1348, wreaked devastation. In the last century, Tilford shed its reliance on agriculture, and with modern means of transport bringing London within commuter distance, it became 'gentrified' and tending to be more like a dormitory village.

The book is divided into chapters which cover the traditional divisions of history and which, of necessity, embrace long periods of time in the early stages. The later chapters correspond broadly with the relevant centuries.

Chapter 1

Facts and Figures

The village of Tilford lies in the Green Belt in the extreme south-west of Surrey, three miles south-east of the town of Farnham. It occupies just under 4 square miles (2439 acres) in an Area of Outstanding Natural Beauty (AONB) and an Area of Great Landscape Value (AGLV). To the east lies the village of Elstead whilst to the south are Rushmoor and Churt and to the south-west, Frensham. Tilford is broadly rectangular in shape with its longer side approximately on a north-east to south-west line and with its centre at the confluence of two branches of the river Wey. The river forms the boundary for part of the way in the north-west and in the south-east, and for a short length in the south-west. At the last count, the village had a population of around 700 (550 electors) in some 240 dwellings.

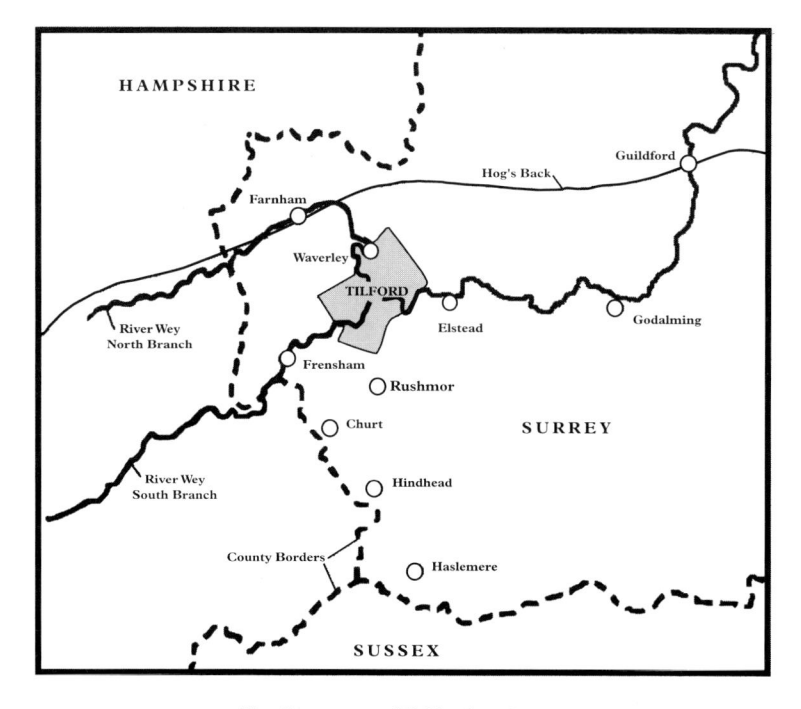

The Location of Tilford in Surrey

The question often asked about Tilford is 'where did it get its name?'. Unfortunately, there is no straightforward answer to this. The spelling of the name has varied over the years. The earliest records of the village refer to it variously as *Tileford, Tilleford, Tylleford, Tolleford* and *Tilforte*. The first appearance of the name on a map was one of Surrey by John Norden in 1594 where it is titled *Tylforde*. A century later, the maps refer to it as *Tylford* - whilst the first map to use the modern spelling appeared in 1760. The bridges at Tilford were of singular importance and for a time the village was marked on the map as *Tylford Bridges* (or just the one word *Bridges*) and this continued as late as 1805. Ordnance Survey maps have always used *Tilford* and this is now the accepted spelling.

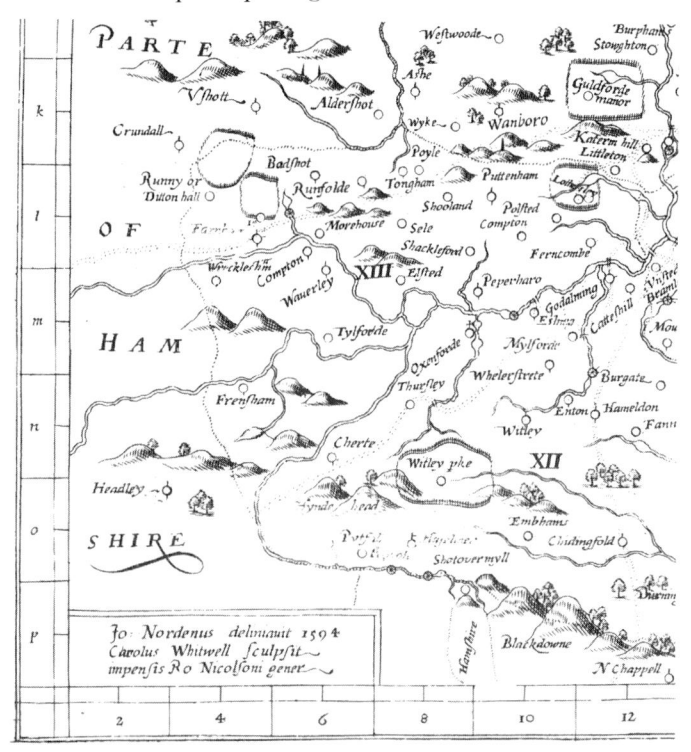

2. Part of Map of Surrey by John Norden 1594
(reproduced by kind permission of Harry Margary Maps, Lympne Castle, Kent, GT21 4LQ).

This map was the first to include the village of 'Tylforde' but Norden is clearly grievously in error over the position of the river Wey. It wasn't until a century later, in John Seller's map of 1690, that the village-this time spelt 'Tylford' - was located in its correct position at the junction of two branches of the river.

Many suggestions have been put forward on the derivation of the name but it has not been possible to agree on any one version. Whilst 'ford' is universally accepted as having its common meaning, there are many interpretations of the 'til' prefix. The first suggestion came in 'Surrey Local Names' published in 1888, in which the author, Gerald S. Davies, maintained that 'til' is the Old English name for lime which is related to the Latin name *tilia*, the lime tree; the obvious implication being that in Saxon times the ford was surrounded by lime trees. In 1900, a local historian, George Gibbons, countered this by the argument that the Saxon word 'til' translated as 'by the station or goal' and probably referred to a marker such as an oak tree which might have been planted on the river bank to commemorate some now forgotten event.

In the authoritative work, the 'Victoria County History of Surrey', published in 1905 and edited by H E Malden, it is posited that "Tilford tithing possibly derived its name from an early manufacture of tiles in the vicinity". Certainly, there is clear evidence of Roman pottery works in Tilford and it is possible that tiles also were produced at these sites. In the 'Place Names of England and Wales' written by the Reverend J. B. Johnston in 1914, another suggestion is put forward - one that has the great merit of simplicity. He concluded that the "name comes from Tila" - the man who either lived by or looked after the ford. The name of the place would then be 'Tila's ford'. Although there is no historical record of a person with the name Tila (or Tilla), later documents indicate that a *virgate* (see glossary) known as 'Tilford' lay to the north of the river next to where the west bridge was to be constructed in the middle ages. Other virgates in the village had their owners' names attached to them and so there are strong arguments in favour of this suggestion.

The same conclusion is reached by three other authorities: 'English Place-Name Elements', by A H Smith published in 1956, the 'Concise Oxford Dictionary of Place-Names' published in 1960, and the 'Place Names of Surrey' by Gover, Mawer and Stenton published in 1982. However, these also include alternative possibilities depending on how the Old English word 'til' is understood. Smith translates it as 'useful' or 'good'; whilst in the Oxford Dictionary it is translated as 'convenient'.

Finally, a number of writers have suggested that the name Tilford indicates the position of a ford across the river Til or Till. However, the use of the   1 term 'til' to describe the river is the invention of 19th century cartographers who wanted to give different names to the two branches of the Wey. It has no historical backing.

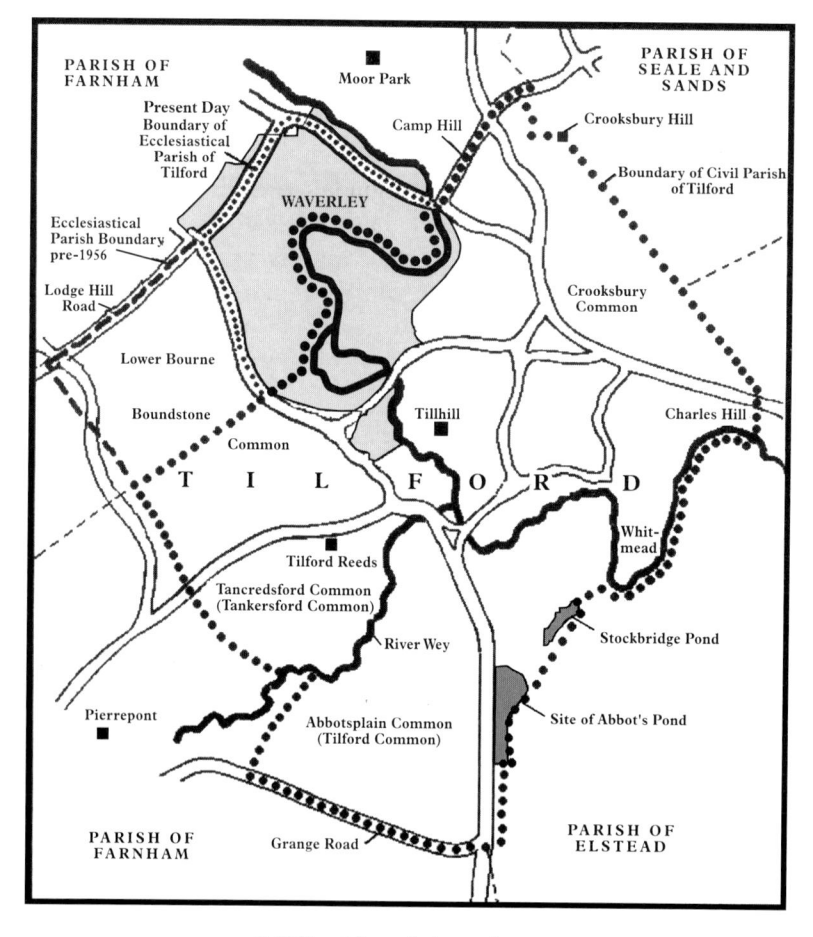

3. Tilford Parish Boundaries

The present-day Civil Parish was established in 1933 and the Ecclesiastical Parish in 1956 when Lower Bourne was transferred to St Thomas Bourne. Before 1894, Waverley was ex parochial and separate from Tilford or Farnham.

As well as difficulty over the name of the village, there is confusion too over what constitutes the administrative area of Tilford. Two separate parishes have to be considered: the civil parish and the ecclesiastical parish. When Farnham Manor was created in the seventh century, Tilford emerged as

4

one of its *tithings* (see glossary). Its boundaries were ill-defined especially so in the north where, later on, Waverley Abbey was to be founded in the 12th century. As parishes began to be formed, and Elstead, Seale and Frensham began to run their own affairs, Tilford's boundaries on the south, east and west began to be formalised; although, with no natural landmarks, the featureless heath gave much room for dispute.

In later years, beating the bounds of Farnham using crosses marked on appropriate stones and trees gave firmer guidance as to where the boundary lay, but it wasn't until the 19th century that these were shown on published maps. To the north of Tilford, the boundary with Waverley was unambiguous, but where Tilford abutted the other tithings of Farnham, Runvale (Runfold) and Dogflud (Bourne) it was only vague.

Tilford became an ecclesiastical parish in its own right in 1865. The area covered was the village itself together with the whole of what is now Lower Bourne and all but a tiny northern part of Waverley Abbey's lands. The northern boundary on the west was Lodge Hill Road and on the east was Camp Hill. The civil parish of Farnham was defined in 1894 under the Local Government Act of that year, and Tilford (encompassing all of the ecclesiastical parish together with Compton and Moor Park), Wrecclesham, and Hale were made 'wards' of a newly-formed Farnham Rural District Council (RDC). As time went on, Farnham Town made repeated inroads into the area covered by the rural designation and by 1924, only a reduced Tilford Ward was left to form Farnham RDC. Finally, in 1933, under the Surrey Review Order of that year, Lower Bourne and the Waverley Abbey lands north of the river were taken away from Tilford and transferred to Farnham; and this, with one slight modification, remains the pattern today. In 1956, the ecclesiastical parish partly followed suit and most of the Lower Bourne was transferred from All Saints Tilford to St Thomas on the Bourne. The whole of Waverley Abbey, however, was retained as part of ecclesiastical Tilford.

To the south of Tilford lies Rushmoor which emerged after the commons were enclosed in 1853. It has a mixture of affiliations, being part of the civil parish of Frensham whilst in the ecclesiastical parish of Churt. Properties close to the border with Tilford have Tilford as their postal address and are sometimes included in the curtilage of the village. In the mid 1950's, there was a move to incorporate Rushmoor into Tilford Parish but following a popular vote amongst the Rushmoor residents, it was eventually decided they should retain the *status quo*.

So that comparisons over time can be consistent, in what follows only figures for the area covered by the present-day civil parish of Tilford have been considered. Up to the middle of the 19th century, this had a negligible effect on the record of population numbers since Waverley's facts and figures could easily be identified and separated from those of Tilford, and the Lower Bourne was waste land and virtually uninhabited. However, later on, many of the statistics - particularly those of the censuses - have to be analysed in detail before the resulting numbers can be said to refer specifically to the area covered by today's village.

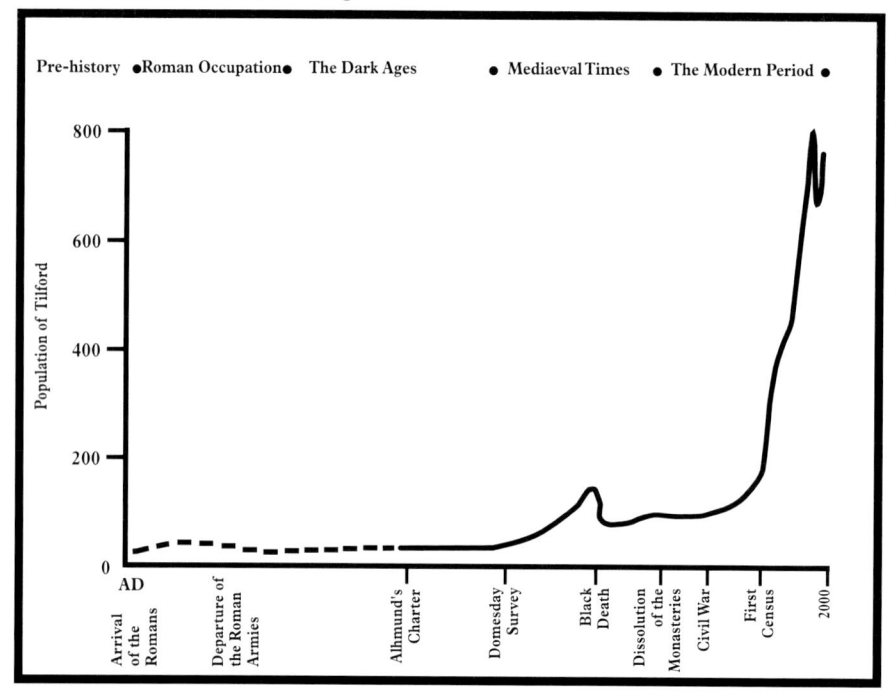

The Population of Tilford

The first national census took place at the start of the 19th century as a result of George III's Population Act of 1800. Before that, population figures have to be assessed from the various returns made to authorities usually for fiscal purposes. Alhmund's Charter of 805 and the Domesday,

Survey of 1086 give figures for Farnham Manor from which some measure of Tilford's population can be gauged. Before that, although we know that the area was occupied in Roman times, only a 'feel' for numbers can be made. The first reliable return giving specific details for Tilford are the 1332 taxation returns; after that, various tax and rent returns, musters and probate records can be used to deduce population figures. Census returns giving details of individuals started in 1841 and from then on, reliable figures for Tilford are available.

Tiny at the dawn of history, Tilford's population increased to around 135 by 1332. The Black Death which followed reduced the population by perhaps as much as a half and levels didn't fully recover for nearly 300 years. By the time of the 1811 census, numbers had reached around 165 and from then on rose steadily, reaching a peak of some 800 in 1971 before falling back to around 700 today.

Chapter 2

Landscape and Land

Tilford is located in the extreme western part of the Weald which embraces the major part of the county of Kent, the whole of Sussex, the southern half of Surrey and a small part of Hampshire. In the west, the Weald starts at Farnham and is bounded on the north by the North Downs. In Tilford, away from the river, it is nearly all sand, although there is one small area of loam south of Stockbridge pond and outcrops of river gravel at Sheephatch and also north of Tilford Reeds. One small deposit of gault clay which was discovered by the Romans near Whitmead was sufficient for them to found a pottery works in the area. Along the river are alluvium deposits for about 100 yards on each side and these provide the fertile soil which made it possible for early man to eke out a living in the area.

The geology of the area is the result of depositions over millions of years. Over much of this time, what was to become the British Isles lay under water and the shifting continents brought the region sometimes nearer the equator and sometimes nearer the north pole. During the time of the dinosaurs, the Weald was a vast lake extending into what is now France. Dominant vertebrates included the plant-eating 26 metres long Diplodocus

5. The Shores of the Wealden Lake 100 million years ago.
(reproduced by permission of the British Geological Survey. © NERC. All rights reserved. IPR/6-22)

and the fish-eating two-tonnes Baronyx whose remains have been found in south-east England. Plant life was made up mainly of conifers, cycads, ferns, and rushes.

Around 100 million years ago, a rise in the level of the sea which lay to the south encroached on to the lake which then became a shallow marine bay in which sand was deposited. Below the sand, loam and clay had been deposited at earlier times and above it, chalk formed later when a relatively shallow sea dominated the area. The chalk was notable for the presence of flint and in the sand, deposits of chert and ironstone occurred in small amounts. In places the sand consolidated to form Bargate stone - a common local building material. About 25 million years ago, during the time of mountain building when the Alps were formed, the land that is now Southern England was folded into a dome and subsequent erosion and the development of the river systems have worn away the chalk at Tilford and have exposed the sand which is now the main surface feature.

The district around Tilford is drained by the river Wey which has two main branches. One rises near Alton and flows in a north-easterly direction through Farnham before turning south along the 'Waverley Valley' to join the other main branch in Tilford. This other branch rises near Selborne and flows in a deep valley which runs in a parallel direction to the first branch. After meeting in Tilford, the combined stream flows eastwards through Godalming to Broadford south of Guildford where it is joined by a third branch before travelling northwards through a gap in the chalk escarpment, finally reaching the Thames at Weybridge.

This was not always the pattern. There is good evidence that some 2 million years ago, there were two parallel streams flowing from south to north. One to the west of Tilford flowing from a region around Headley through a gap in the chalk at Crondall; and the other flowing through Tilford through a second gap at Aldershot. Around six hundred thousand years ago, as the dome over the Weald further shifted and eroded, the western stream turned north eastwards and was 'captured' by the eastern stream just before it went through the Aldershot gap. The combined stream became the Blackwater river. Meanwhile, a new river was becoming established that would eventually become the Selborne-Godalming part of the Wey. This took all the water passing through Tilford which consequently left the Waverley Valley empty. Finally, the Aldershot gap became redundant as what was before the Blackwater river found an easier way through the Waverley Valley, this time travelling southwards, where it joined the established Wey to form the present arrangement.

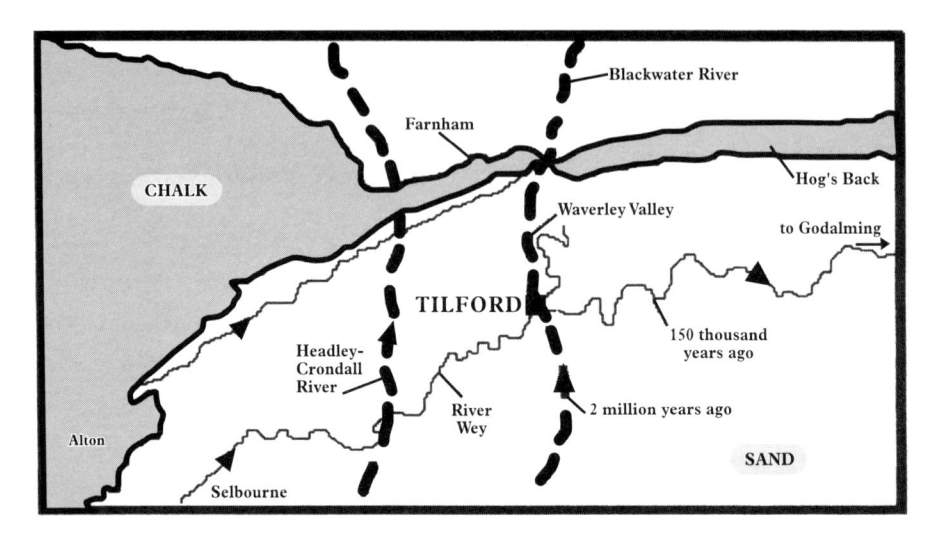

6. Change in the Course of the River Wey over the last two million years.

Whilst the latter stages of these changes were taking place, palaeolithic (or old stone age) man appeared on the scene. He was not modern man but was nevertheless a member of the human race. By the time modern humans arrived, some 40,000 years ago, geological conditions were very much the same as now. Not so the climate. The world had then just recovered from one of its great ice ages and would be preparing to embark on one very much colder - an ice age which ended some 10,000 years ago and one from which we are still moving away. This period saw the emergence of mesolithic (or middle stone age) man, to be followed, in a relatively short time compared with the previous intervals, by neolithic (or new stone age) man and then the bronze and iron ages.

Chapter 3

Prehistoric Tilford

Whilst geology speaks in terms of millions of years, archaeology covers hundreds of thousands. In considering the prehistory of Tilford, from the time man entered Surrey until the time of the Romans, we are concerned with a period of 500,000 years; and for 470,000 of those years, we are dealing with human beings related to, but very different from, modern man. Such early peoples of the Palaeolithic, or old stone, age travelled in the south of England in small foraging bands when climatic conditions allowed. For much of the time, the earth was in the grip of a series of ice ages lasting many thousands of years separated by only relatively short periods of warmth. For this very long period, the human race showed very little change, marked only by improvements in the ways the flint stones used as tools were fashioned.

Into the area which was to become Tilford, early stone age man would have ventured from the continent when the climate became milder, retreating again when climatic conditions became intolerable. For most of the time it was cold, and treeless tundra would have covered the land. Remains from the Palaeolithic period are rare in S.E. England and up to the end of the 19th century, only the Thames valley had yielded any appreciable artefacts from this period. Since then, four have been discovered in Tilford and many more in the gravel beds close to Farnham. In all, Surrey has 124 sites at which Palaeolithic flints have been found. With the great climatic and geological changes that occurred over the Palaeolithic period of man's prehistory, it is difficult to form any valid conclusions on his occupation of the Tilford area. However, the finds at Farnham cover the full time span - ranging from 472,000 years ago to 13,000 years, and so it is very likely that Tilford, with all its geological, climatic, floral and faunal upheavals, was part of man's territory for the whole of the Palaeolithic period.

Towards the end of this very long time span, modern man appeared on the scene. It is difficult to imagine what Tilford must have been like at this time. Human numbers were absurdly low and the prehistoric people were nomads, forever on the move, engaged in hunting wild animals, fishing, and gathering the natural fruits of the earth. As he emerges from the Palaeolithic period, some 10,000 years ago - at the start of the Mesolithic, or middle stone, age - man's mark on the land becomes clearer and the story of Tilford really begins. This was the time when Britain was emerging from the last ice age and the woodlands were beginning to creep back to take over from the tundra and moorland which had occupied all of the land south of the glaciers. With so much water locked up in continental ice, sea levels remained low and Britain was still connected to the continental mainland facilitating modern man's westward journey to Britain from the land of his origins.

The first trees to arrive, between 11,000 and 8,000 B.C. were the birch, pine and hazel followed by the alder and willow. Next came the lime, elm, oak, and finally the ash, beech, holly, hornbeam and maple. Altogether, although punctuated by glades maintained by browsing animals, they formed a dense, sometimes impenetrable, forest covering over two thirds of Britain. The woodlands were at their most dense on clay soils and the Weald must have been particularly difficult to penetrate. The lighter soils around the Farnham area would have favoured a mixture of oak and hazel and would have been the preferred area for food-gathering and hunting by nomadic man, with the river Wey providing a convenient and fruitful avenue of travel. It is therefore not surprising that it is along this river that we find so many Mesolithic remains.

In Tilford, in particular, a great many artefacts have been discovered, principally by the reverend Edge who, when vicar of Tilford from 1885 to 1929, made many excursions around the parish looking for remains from this period. His finds, which now form the Edge collection in Guildford Museum, include stone arrowheads, scrapers, knives and axes - all collected, according to the reverend Edge, 'within a mile of Tilford Church'. Many of such finds were made in Chapel Field which is recognised as a major site for Mesolithic industry and one on which hut sites from this period have been identified. Indeed the site has been described as 'the most imposing example of a river bluff plateau settlement in the region' linking, along the Wey, with what was once thought to be a major pit-dwelling site at Farnham near Bourne Mill.

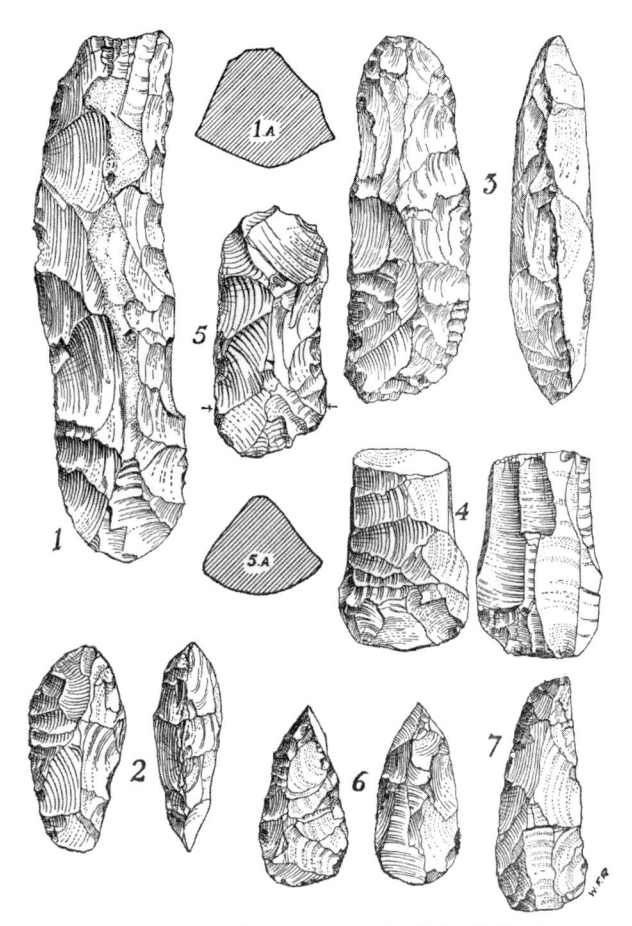

7. Mesolithic Tranchet Axes from the Edge Collection
(reproduced by kind permission of the Surrey Archaeological Society, Castle Arch, Guildford, GU1 3SX)

1, 3 & 5 ~ Flint picks from Ware Reeds
2, 4, 6 & 7 ~ Flint adzes from Malt House Field

Other Mesolithic finds have been made all round Tilford: in the fields close by the Malthouse, on Crooksbury summit, at Sheephatch, on Hankley Common, at Stonehills, and on land to the east of Stockbridge pond just across the boundary into Elstead. They continue to be made today.

Around 6,500 years ago, the Mesolithic peoples were succeeded by those of the Neolithic or new stone age. It was at this time that farming began to be adopted; the nomadic way of life of the Mesolithic people gave way to agriculture, areas of woodlands and scrub started to be cleared away, and great ritual and burial monuments were constructed. Whilst there is no direct evidence of this activity at Tilford, archaeological remains consisting of axes, arrowheads, scrapers and other tools from the Neolithic period have been discovered in and around the village. The Neolithic folk selected dry, sandy slopes with southern aspect near rivers, pools, or springs for their camps and the nature of the Wey valley, which has yielded the greatest number of finds, was clearly much favoured.

As numbers grew and travel and communications between groups became more common, improvements in technology became more widespread. A common style of pottery, identified by a distinctive decoration on beakers, began to be adopted in Europe around 4,500 years ago accompanied by an understanding of the manufacture of bronze, that ushered in the so-called Bronze Age. Although the advantages of bronze led to many implements being made of this metal, this was not universal and stone continued to be used where materials were not available and metal-working was not practicable. However, stone implements and weapons such as the barbed and tanged arrowheads which superseded the leaf-shaped ones of Neolithic man, were generally of improved design.

Evidence of beaker pottery is virtually non-existent in Surrey but many other Bronze Age artefacts have been discovered in the region. The Edge collection, for example, contains some 100 such pieces from Tilford. A hoard of bronze implements and weapons was discovered at Crooksbury in 1857, some pieces from which are in the Guildford Museum; and another small hoard was found on Hankley Common. At Birchen Reeds, a socketed knife has been discovered and a sickle flint from this period has also been found. In addition to these implements and weapons there are a number of significant earthworks to be seen in the area such as the one at Crooksbury Common which presents a fine example of a bronze age earthwork in its Triple Bell Barrow consisting of 3 mounds of earth enclosed by a single ditch. Such barrows were the burial grounds of important Bronze Age people and usually contain cremated bones placed in an earthen pot, very occasionally accompanied by a bronze tool such as an axe or dagger.

The Crooksbury barrows have an external bank varying in height from 2 to

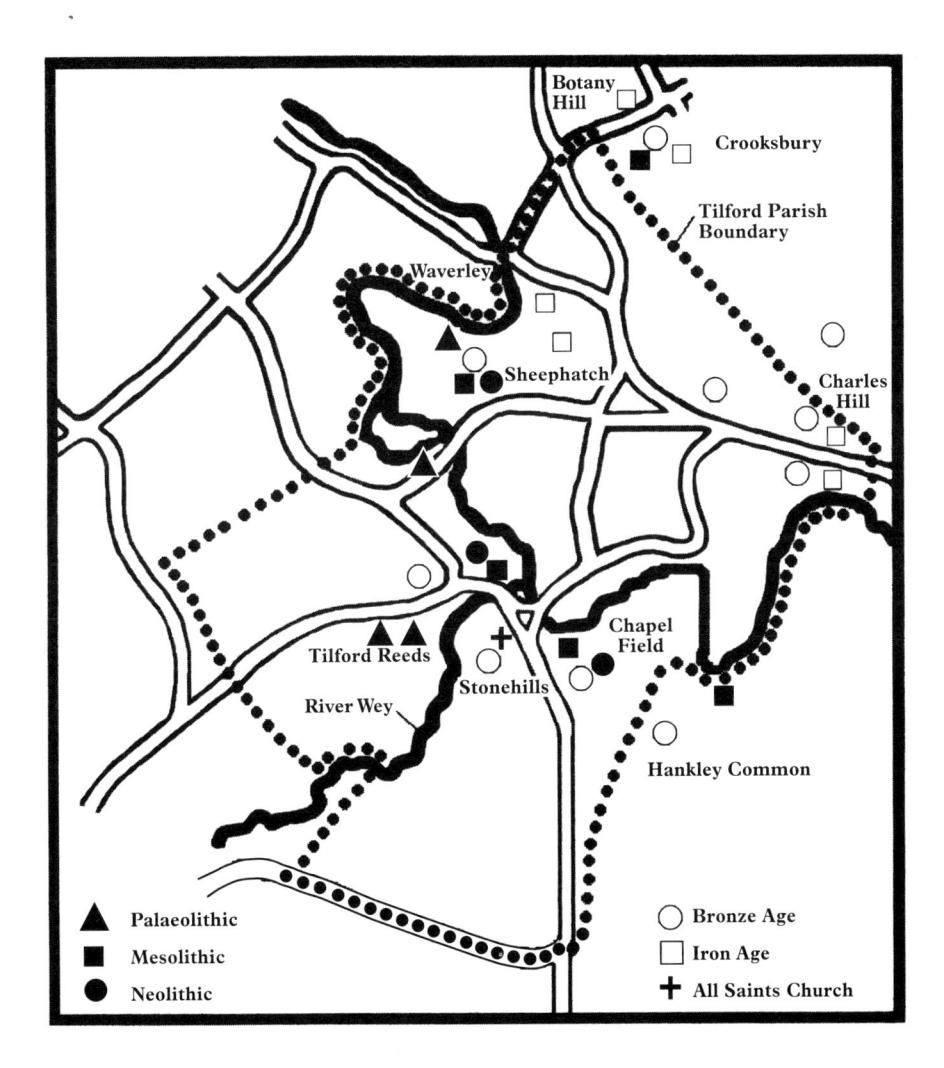

8. Prehistoric Remains in Tilford.

Tilford's prehistoric remains cover all periods from the Stone Age to the Iron Age indicating that its location at the confluence of two rivers made it an attractive site for early man.

3 metres and in diameter from 9 to 18 metres and lie just outside the Tilford boundary, north of Charles Hill. There are other important barrows around Frensham Pond where much excavation work has been

done recently but the barrows at Crooksbury have yet to be looked at closely and their secrets remain intact. Charles Hill is the site of other important tumuli of this period including a line of five barrows at the rear of the present-day Tilford Barrows house which were scheduled under the Ancient Monuments Act of 1913. For a long time largely overgrown, they are currently being cleared of the trees and bushes which have all but hidden them from view.

During the later Bronze Age, around 1600 B.C., there was a sudden explosion in the population of England which increased, over a few centuries, from some thirty to forty thousand to as many as a million; numerous new settlements appeared and fields and field systems emerged. The barrows at Tilford imply that a local settlement had been established at this time. This, however, may not have been permanent since there is good evidence that such settlements moved constantly over the centuries.

The Iron Age, which followed around 1000 B.C., showed no sudden break in continuity and it is often difficult to discriminate between late Bronze Age and early Iron Age earthworks. Those in Tilford ascribed to the later period (but over which there remains much controversy) include the earthwork at Botany Hill and the ancient British camp called 'The Soldiers' Ring' close to the summit of Crooksbury Hill. Both consist of circular enclosures with a single ditch and rampart. The 'Soldier's Ring', which is the better preserved, is about 50 metres in diameter. An 'entrenchment' used to be recorded on the Ordnance Survey maps as crossing the Elstead Road from north to south near to Tilford Barrows at Charles Hill. Present day maps continue to show where this might have been but its origins and purpose remains unclear. Some writers have conjectured that the 'entrenchment' might have been confused with the barrow mounds nearby, but this does not appear to be likely.

In 1895, the upper stone of a British quern or hand-mill (but lacking its nether-stone) dating back to this time was discovered some 700 metres to the north east of Sheephatch and close by are some man-made ditches believed to be of this period. Other earthworks of uncertain origin have been found around Tilford, such as the embankment which used to be in the field south of the Reeds Road some 400 metres from its junction with Tilford Road which was identified as of archaeological interest but is now grubbed up; and similar earthworks (2 metres high and $6^{1}/_{2}$ metres wide) which, as were earlier reported, lie along Whitmead Lane - apparently erected to protect a camp on the adjoining high ground north of the present-day Archers Hill house.

The increased numbers of people during the Bronze Age and Iron Age led to the destruction of much of the original wildwood that dominated the landscape in ancient times. Palaeolithic and Mesolithic men had axes and would have made temporary clearings in the forests but their numbers were so small that they would have made little impact overall. Destruction of the wildwood for cultivation began in the Neolithic age but accelerated over the Bronze and Iron Age periods. It has been estimated that half of England had ceased to be wildwood by 500 BC. In Surrey, such devastation of the woods on the greensand soils produced the heathlands which, because of continuous grazing, have persisted up to the present day.

The mass of archaeological evidence clearly shows that the Wey Valley was attractive to prehistoric man. It is not difficult to see why. The presence of springs, streams and the river would have provided essential drinking water and the Wey would have been a valuable source of fish and a means of transport; the widely-spread flood-plains and alluvial deposits would have sustained a variety of plants, and accessibility to flint in the chalk outcrops close by would have given the necessary material for producing stone tools and implements. Initially well wooded, the outlying trees, thanks to man's insatiable rapacity, eventually gave way to less hospitable surrounding heathland. Even so there would have been enough cover, building material, and fuel from the woodlands closer in to enable families to survive and later on to develop a farming community. Although variable in quality, the nearby warm greensand would be well-drained and easily ploughed and was able to provide reasonably fertile soil for the growing of crops and the grazing of animals.

Situated at the confluence of its two rivers, Tilford had all these advantages and was well placed for human habitation. As we shall see in the next chapter, there is evidence of pottery manufacture at a later date in Tilford showing that the area supported local industry. As we move to the Roman period, when historical records first start to appear, we can assume with some confidence that Tilford had already, for some while, been a productive place of settlement.

Chapter 4

The Roman Occupation

From A.D. 43 to about A.D. 410, Britain south of Hadrian's Wall was under Roman rule. Caesar had invaded in 55 B.C. and had found an island with an "exceedingly large population, the ground thickly studded with homesteads, closely resembling the Gauls, and the cattle very numerous.....the climate more temperate than in Gaul, the cold being less severe". Whilst these observations of Caesar were focused principally on what he encountered in Kent, conditions in the countryside along the North and South Downs would not have differed greatly from these and we can safely assume that Tilford in south-west Surrey would have been part of a settled and prospering land.

The country was split into regions or kingdoms which originated from the people of different tribes who had invaded Britain over the previous two centuries. Surrey straddled the border of the *Cantiaci* tribe in the east and the *Atrebates* tribe in the west. The tribal boundary between them is a matter of speculation. It has been suggested that the boundary actually fell along the Wey Valley. If so, Tilford would have been in a position of some importance and possible confrontation. However, there is no clear evidence of this - major actions were focused on the Thames Valley where powerful warlike tribes to the north were at odds with their southern neighbours - a confrontation which Caesar tried unsuccessfully to exploit when he invaded Britain in 55 and 54 B.C. By the time of the Roman conquest under Claudius in A.D. 43, Cunobelinus, King of Essex, had become 'Overlord' of the south and was being referred to as 'King of Britain'.

Although the Romans were engaged in many local actions before conquering the south of England, there are few military remains in Surrey dating from this time compared with elsewhere, suggesting a low level of warlike engagements here. This continued throughout the Roman occupation and as H.E. Malden has concluded in his 'History of Surrey', all the indications are that, under the Romans, Surrey was 'a pleasant, rural country, ungarrisoned and secure from enemies, during the greater part of the Imperial rule'.

Communications were, and still are, the key to development. London on the Thames waterway became the focus of Roman activity and roads were built stretching out to all parts of the kingdom. Four such roads have been identified as crossing Surrey and others have been conjectured and await further investigation. London and Winchester would most likely have been

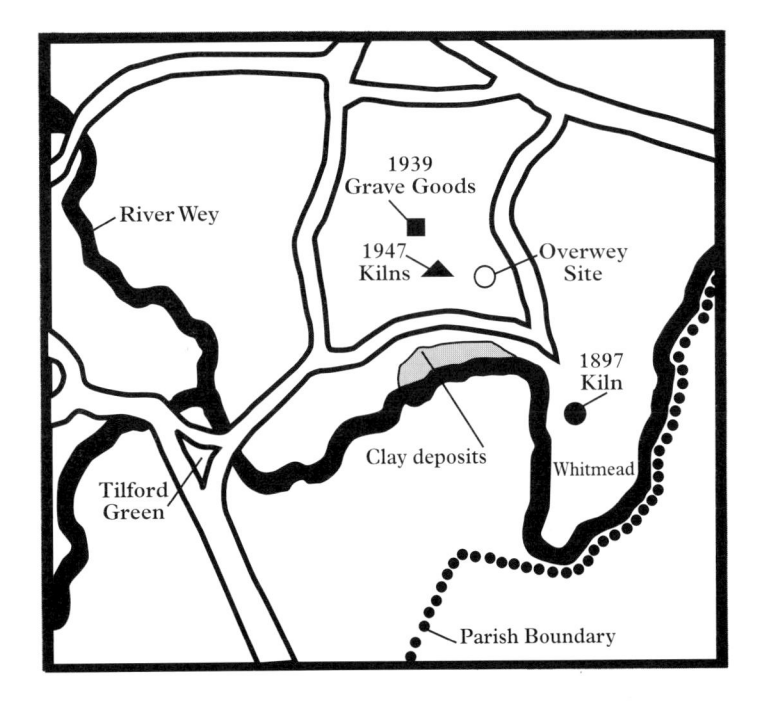

9. Roman Remains in Tilford.

The pottery kilns at Tilford comprise an extension eastwards from the local Roman pottery industrial complex which was centred at Alice Holt.

connected by a Roman road and the route of such a road has been traced from Winchester to Farnham following roughly that of the modern A31. The route from Farnham to London, however, still remains unclear. The river Wey, on the other hand, provided a sure connection with the Thames and hence with London, and this is likely to have been a valued means of transport in late Roman times and afterwards, although the full extent of its use is controversial.

Life in Tilford at this time is obscure but there is telling evidence of a pottery industry. This flourishing business is thought to have been centred around Farnham extending into Alice Holt which, because it later became a mediaeval hunting forest, has remained undisturbed over a long period of time. Many remains from the Roman period have survived in this area and much evidence of Roman pottery manufacture has been discovered. The Farnham/Alice Holt potters produced coarse, grey, kitchen wares with large-scale production taking place from about A.D. 60 to the fifth century.

Evidence for a pottery works in Tilford was first established in 1897 when a kiln purported to be dating from Roman or British times was found at Whitmead. At the time, it was reported that the kiln was about 4 feet under the soil, was 8 feet long by 4 feet wide, and was floored with Roman tiles. Unfortunately, the kiln was destroyed shortly afterwards and in the absence of any pottery at the site, there has been some question about its authenticity. A more reliable piece of evidence was brought to light in 1937 when, in an area littered with potsherds, a trial trench at Overwey in Tilford revealed a structure whose sides were lined with rough sandstone blocks. The site lay forgotten during the Second World War but at the beginning of 1947, at the instigation of the then owner of Overwey, the late Major C.W. De Roemer, a new trench was dug revealing an oven and a large quantity of pottery.

10. A Roman Jar From 'Overwey' in Tilford
(reproduced by kind permission of the late Martin C. De Roemer, Overwey, Tilford)

This attractive jar was discovered in Tilford during excavations at 'Overwey' in 1947. The 'bands' on the jar are in different shades of grey, typical of the products produced at the Roman potteries in Tilford during the fourth century A.D.

As a result of these finds a full-scale excavation of the whole site by members of the Surrey Archaeological Society was started in May 1947. About half-way through, the excavators were reinforced by parties of children from Sheephatch School who undertook much of the heavy work on the site. Three kilns were found occupying two distinct sites on either side of a gulley which ran down to the river 1,100 feet away; this gulley was thought to have been formed by a spring emanating close to the kilns thus providing the necessary water supply. A suitable source of clay was found close by the river and there was a good supply of wood for fuel. The kilns each of overall length 15 feet and maximum width 4 feet consisted of a central oven with a furnace at each end, the walls of which were constructed of large sandstone and ironstone blocks mortared with clay. Above the walls it is most likely that the roofs were closed with turves; access to each of the furnaces was gained by stoke pits, one at each outer end.

The pottery produced in Tilford comprised mainly cooking jars, storage jars, flasks, bowls and dishes of which the most common was the cooking jar. The prevailing colour was grey although some of the wares were pink and buff. In the very early stages, much Farnham/Alice Holt pottery was sold in London and it has been suggested that transport for this would have been by shallow barge along the Wey. Although such barges from this country have yet to be found, the remains of Roman barges on the Rhine provide examples of the type of boat that have been used in shallow water.

Air photography and fieldwork have revealed short lengths of road running south from the Alice Holt centres to the north bank of the river Slea and it has been suggested that pottery was loaded on to the barges at these points as the river, it is said, was navigable. The Slea runs into the southern Wey which combines with the northern Wey at Tilford and we can imagine such barges being towed through Tilford on their way to the Thames and London taking the Overwey pottery on board as they passed through on their way to the Capital.

London was not the only destination for Farnham/Alice Holt pottery. Locally, the produce sold well in north-east Hampshire, north-west Sussex and south-west Surrey and the urban centres of Winchester and Silchester absorbed much of the output. As the centuries advanced, Farnham/Alice Holt pottery was used increasingly as containers for the local produce that needed to be transported and it thus achieved wide distribution. It is estimated that in the late fourth century, Farnham/Alice Holt pottery dominated the London pottery market and Tilford's pottery industry would have been kept busy meeting the demand.

It is suspected that other Roman pottery works still remain to be found in Tilford. In 1939, twenty-two pottery vessels were discovered at a depth of eighteen inches at a site some 300 yards north of the Overwey kiln and these are believed to be grave goods associated with a cremation burial and date from the third quarter of the first century A.D. The kilns at the Overwey site, on the other hand, are reckoned to have been in operation over the fourth century A.D. Other Roman finds in Tilford include a series of ditches or sunken tracks at Sheephatch just south of Waverley Mill and an Egyptian *Ushabti* figure of the time of Rameses II discovered on the surface of a field near the river together with some Romano-British pottery. It is surmised that this was either lost by a Roman soldier who had visited Egypt or an Egyptian in the service of Rome.

11. Egyptian 'Ushabti' found in Tilford
(reproduced by kind permission of the Surrey Archaeological Society, Castle Arch, Guildford, GU1 3SX)

The Egyptian '*Ushabti*' depicted was found in 1908 on the surface of a field near the river Wey at Tilford alongside pieces of Romano-British pottery. '*Ushabti*' is the name given to a little statuette and means the '*Answerer*', a figure that was placed in a grave so that when the owner 'awakened' he could compel the '*Ushabti*' to do work for him.

Overall, such finds suggest that there was a continuous human presence in Tilford during the Roman occupation and raises the question of how the pottery works were supported. The pottery workers were perhaps specialists supported by a permanent farming settlement already established in Tilford. Alternatively, they may have been part-time potters with some sort of agricultural holding as well. The dwellings occupied by the inhabitants of such a settlement would have been so insubstantial that it would be surprising if any survived; certainly no remains of such structures have yet been found in Tilford. The remains of a Roman Dwelling and Bath House dating from between A.D. 250 and 400 have, however, been discovered in Farnham on what is now known as the 'Roman Way Estate'. Excavations in 1946/47 revealed an aqueduct and the foundations of two buildings. It has been suggested that the bath house had been erected for the use of pottery workers and that the dwelling was a small house possibly occupied by the 'manager' of the nearby pottery works but this has been questioned. Such structures may yet be found in Tilford.

As we move towards the end of the period of Roman occupation of Britain we can speculate on how Tilford was faring. After three and a half centuries of occupation, many of the Romans and other 'foreigners' brought in by them would have integrated with the native population. As more and more of the Roman Empire came under attack, the 'crack' troops of the Roman army would have had to be withdrawn to meet the threat; but military units lower down the scale would probably have been left at their posts, and they and their wives and children with them would have become part of the village community.

The fierce barbarian raids which affected the south of Britain around A.D. 368 may well have persuaded some of the Tilford villagers to retreat to the relative safety of other places away from the Farnham area - placed as this area was on the main east-west, London to Winchester, route - but others would have been expected to remain. It is possible that the pattern of division of land that we see embedded in Norman times originated over this period.

The upheaval caused by the withdrawal of the Roman troops and the decline of the Roman Empire led to a rapid fall in the pottery trade, and the Overwey kilns, after a long period of use, were apparently peacefully dismantled and filled in with the accumulation of burnt sand and wasters that lay around them in order that the site could be used for agriculture, underlining the stability and continuity of this activity. With the ending of the pottery industry in Tilford, we leave behind what little archaeological evidence there is for life in the village and move on to the Dark Ages and the period where records become so fragmentary that speculation often becomes our only means of presenting history.

Chapter 5

The Dark Ages

Following the departure of the Roman field army from Britain early in the fifth century, the country lay open to invasion and migration. Successive waves of Angles, Saxons, Jutes and later, Vikings came across the channel and the North Sea to settle in Britain, sometimes peaceably and sometimes by force. With its proximity to the continental mainland, the south-east of England was easily reached but compared with other parts, Surrey was less attractive than most. Away from the rivers the soil was not highly productive, dense forests occupied much of the land, and there was no outlet to the sea.

Throughout the whole of the south-east, population densities had been falling since their height in the second and third centuries and had reached new lows. There would have been no lack of choice of land for settlement and it is likely that, initially, the Farnham area including Tilford, surrounded as it was by marsh and heath, would have had relatively few permanent inhabitants. Archaeological remains from this period in the area are notoriously difficult to find. The Saxons, who first came to Surrey were by nature individualists and sought to settle in dispersed farms rather than in nucleated villages. They left little associated pottery, and archaeological evidence of their settlements is very rare. Very little has been discovered in Surrey as a whole. From only one site in the Farnham district has there been any recorded discovery from the early Saxon period, and in Tilford there is none.

Surrey's name comes from the Saxon *Suthrige* meaning southern province. To the south, in Sussex, were the South Saxons; to the west, in Wessex, the West Saxons; and to the north-west the Mercians whose territory extended across the country to Wales. Throughout the whole of the early and middle Saxon period, Surrey was a frontier land buffeted between the rulers of southern England. At times, such as in 568 when the king of Wessex, Ceawlin, drove his foes across Surrey into Kent, war raged from west to east; at other times, such as in 675 when the Mercians established the 'Under-King' Frithuwald in Surrey, the armies crossed from North to South.

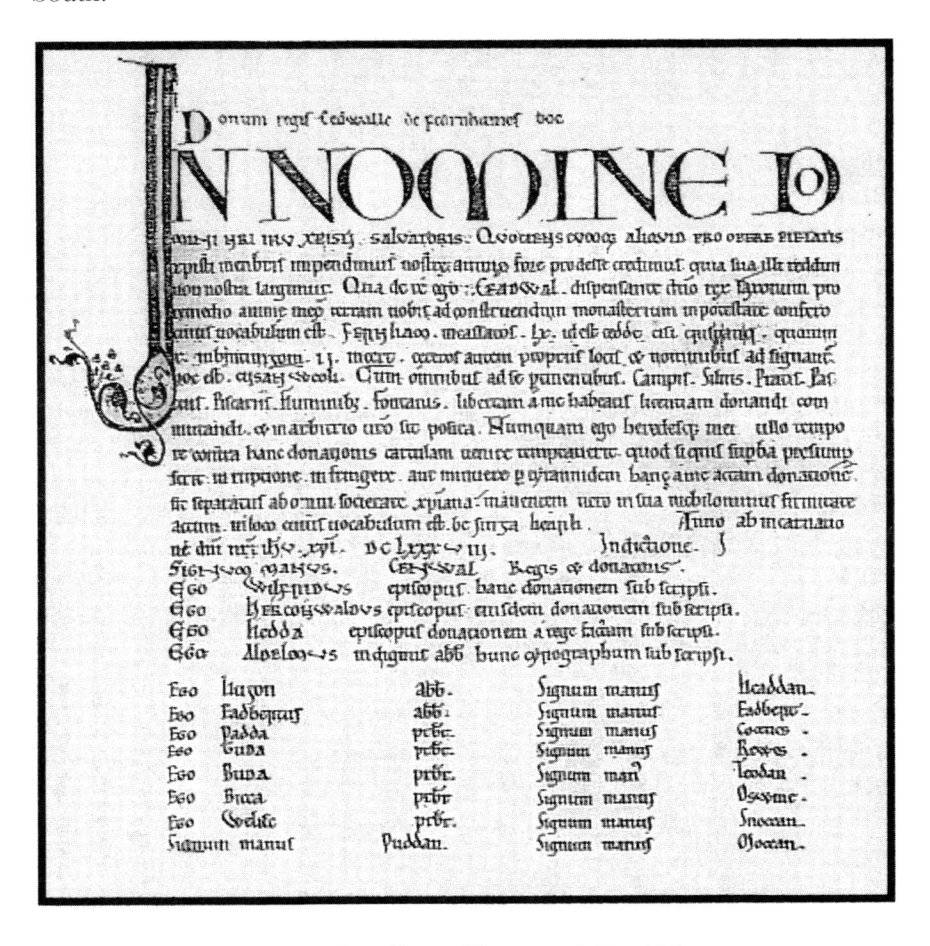

12. Caedwalla's Charter A.D. 688
(reproduced by permission of the British Library, ADD.15350 f57v)

Caedwalla's Charter was the first in a series of five known Anglo-Saxon charters relating to Farnham. Caedwalla was King of the Saxons and the charter documents his gift of Farnham Manor to the Christian Church.

The battles between the warring factions reached a critical stage in the late 680's. In 685, according to the Anglo-Saxon Chronicles, a young member of the royal house of Wessex named Caedwalla 'began to contend for the

25

kingdom'. He had an ambition to add all of south-east England to his realm and fought an incessant war over his reign of three years. Towards the end of this time he drew up a charter which gave to a group of Christians the land at Farnham together with its 'fields, woods, meadows, pastures, fisheries, rivers, springs' to found a *monasterium*. This is the first mention of Farnham in the records and the inclusion of human constructs such as meadows and pastures in the description confirms the existence of established habitation and farming that would have originated at a much earlier date.

The form of the wording in the charter together with its signatories underlines the authority of the document and reinforces the belief in the existence of an orderly system of administration at that time. Such a system was based on the *hide*, which was an area of around 120 acres (depending on the quality of the soil) which could be ploughed in a year using a team of eight oxen. Typically, an underling with two oxen would be allocated a *virgate* of land (equal to a quarter of a *hide* or 30 acres). The *hundred* comprised 100 *hides* and was divided into ten *tithings*. The Farnham Estate was identified with 60 *hides* of productive land (used for tax assessment purposes) and was later regarded as one of the Surrey *hundreds* with Tilford as one of its *tithings*.

The exact meaning of the word *monasterium* is not altogether clear; neither has the real purpose behind the gift been adequately surmised. It has been suggested that Caedwalla may have intended the area to be a bulwark between Wessex and any invaders from the East. However, perhaps no political motive was intended and Caedwalla merely aimed to placate his conscience, bearing in mind his previous background of merciless aggression and his travel to Rome in 689 for baptism by the Pope ten days before he died. The reference to *cusan weoh* in the charter, which translates as 'the [heathen] temple of Cusa', supports the existence of pagan worship in the area and Caedwalla's purpose in giving this land to the Christians may have been to support them in mopping up a persistent enclave of paganism.

The *monasterium* was probably intended to be some form of Minster or home for a few priests who would administer the sacraments around the Farnham Estate. The position to be occupied by the *monasterium* is similarly in doubt. Traditionally, it has been associated with St Andrew's Church in the town of Farnham, which, indeed, has fragmentary evidence of Saxon construction. However, there is no reason to suppose that at the time of

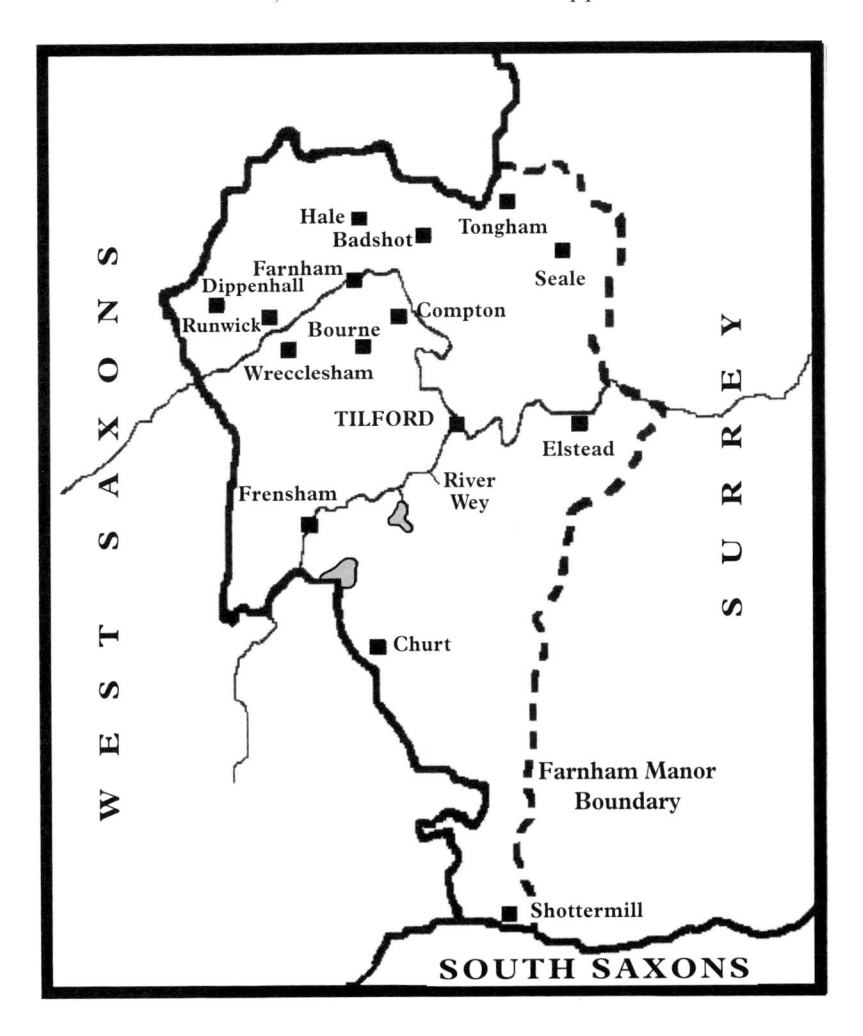

13. The Bounds of Farnham Manor

The bounds of Farnham Manor were set out in A.D. 909 in the Charter of King Edward the Elder (A.D. 901-925) in which he confirmed its ownership by the church to Frithstan, Bishop of Winchester

Caedwalla's charter a formal settlement had been founded on the site of present-day Farnham, and it has been argued that a position in the centre of the Farnham Estate, say at Frensham, would have been more logical place for the founding of a *monasterium*.

How long the *monasterium* lasted we do not know, but by A.D. 805, we find the estate in the hands of the Bishop of Winchester as one of his manors. Somewhere around this year, Alhmund, Bishop of Winchester resolved to exchange Farnham Manor with a person called Byrhtelm for land in Wiltshire and summarised the agreement in a charter. In it he refers to sixty tenants (ie heads of households) occupying the manor and from this, assuming an average of, say, five people in each household, it is possible to estimate a population of around 300 at this time. The extent of the manor can best be gauged from a later charter of Edward the Elder made in A.D. 909. In this, Edward, King of the Anglo-Saxons, endorses the church's ownership of Farnham Manor and includes details of its boundary. This went eleven miles from Caesar's Camp in the north to the Sussex border in the south and five and a half miles from Willey in the west to Elstead in the east an area of some 37 square miles.

By the end of the seventh century, although the south-east had been converted to Christianity and the church was increasingly able to impose its authority on the people, changes in kingship continued to cause upheaval. Caedwalla's success in dominating the south-east had been short-lived and early in the eighth century West Saxon rule was replaced by that of the Mercians. A century later, these, in turn, gave way once again to men from Wessex and from the victory of Ecgbert of Wessex in 825, when the men of Surrey submitted to him, this county was decisively part of his territory.

Into this arena, at the end of the eighth century, came the Vikings from Scandinavia. At first, consisting solely of raiding parties, at length, the invaders stayed for long periods in the country, eventually dominating large areas. By the 880's they occupied Northumbria, Mercia and East Anglia - and the south-east, although not conquered, remained subject to raiding. In order to protect the country, the West Saxons under Alfred constructed a series of fortified centres or *burhs* to act as refuges for the population. Two are known in Surrey, Southwark and Eashing, with the latter later being taken over by Guildford.

14. Postulated Site of the 'Battle of Farnham' A.D. 893

This version of the 'Battle of Farnham' was first advanced by George Gibbons in 1896 in letters to the Surrey & Hants News of December 15th and 21st. In support of his ideas he alluded to Saxon names to the north of the river Wey and Danish names to the south.

In 892, after 15 years of peace, a large body of Vikings assembled in Boulogne to invade England. Two fleets of ships, totalling 330 in all, set out; one fleet landing the Viking army near Folkestone, the other sailing up the Thames. The Danes who had previously settled on the East Coast joined them and together they made their way westwards eventually reaching Hampshire and Berkshire. Turning back to link up with the other force that had deployed along the Essex coast, they were met by the Wessex militia under Edward, Alfred's eldest son, and decisively routed. In the Anglo-Saxon Chronicle this is recorded as the 'Battle of Farnham'.

Exactly where the battle took place has been a subject of much discussion. A very plausible argument has been put forward claiming that it was in Tilford. According to this account, the Danes came up from the south to meet the Saxons advancing from Farnham in the north. The opposing lines kept to the high ground with the Saxons along the range of hills from Millbridge to Elstead north of the Wey and the Danes encamped on the range of hills from Charles Hill though Truxford and Churt to Millbridge. Substance is added to this claim by the existence of an encampment, thought to be Danish, at Longdown and places with Danish names to the south of the village compared with Saxon names to the north. Since there is no evidence that Tilford was ever a Danish settlement (so the argument goes) the Danish names could only have originated from some major event taking place at this location. The 'King's Oak' by the side of the Farnham Road at Tilford, quoted 250 years later as a marker for the bounds of Waverley Abbey, is presumed to have been planted - or at least marked out - to commemorate the Saxon victory.

With the Danes soundly defeated, the country remained at peace for nearly a hundred years under a succession of strong West Saxon rulers. However, in 994, Sweyn of Denmark and Olaf of Norway began a series of attacks which never wholly ceased until Sweyn's son, Canute was recognised as king of England in 1017. During this time, hostile armies traversed Surrey using the London-Winchester road and the families in the Farnham area who had established themselves during the times of peace must have had to suffer much intimidation and harassment as the soldiers passed through their lands.

As we approach 1066 and the Norman invasion, we can stand back and look at Tilford over the six and a half centuries that had passed since the withdrawal of the Roman armies and see a land that supported just a few peasants and their families in their allocated *virgates* close by the river. Such peasants, who were originally pagan but who were later converted to

Christianity, were a mixture of the Romano-British who had flourished during the Roman occupation and the people who had come from Scandinavia to colonise the land. They lived in a 'frontier' state. Wars swept across them at intervals but very little else would have interrupted the harsh and monotonous conditions under which they and their predecessors would have always had to live and work. Later on in the period, the Bishop of Winchester held sway in the Farnham Hundred and the lives of those who settled there were under his protection and rule. For this he demanded allegiance and the payment of rents and taxes. Towards the end of the ninth century the settlement at Tilford was firmly administered by the bishop with all the land owned and let out by him.

Peasant habitations were constructed of such impermanent materials that they would have left little mark on the landscape; and this applies to the whole of Tilford's previous history. With more intensive searching and given the necessary resources, evidence of such habitations remain to be found, but in the absence of this, we are forced back on to speculation, surmise, and inference. It is only with the arrival of the Normans, with their superior administration and record keeping, that we are able to break out of the 'Dark Ages' and gain a more reliable insight into the people of Tilford and the way that they lived.

Chapter 6

The Coming of the Normans

With the coming of William the Conqueror in 1066, many more detailed records begin to be kept, and a more cogent history can be written. The earliest and best known of such records is the Survey stemming from the Domesday Inquest of 1086. This far-reaching document is far from perfect and has to be carefully interpreted. Nevertheless, it has no parallel earlier or elsewhere and contains much invaluable information. Although Surrey was not so well served as other counties (it had no bishop of its own, with no great town, and did not even contain the seat of a Norman earl or great baron), the document still contains lists of all the land holdings and their occupiers, together with an assessment of their value. Farnham Manor - as at least five Saxon Charters had earlier confirmed - belonged to the Bishop of Winchester and as Domesday observed: "The Bishop of Winchester holds Farnham. Saint Peter always held it." With Winchester the seat of the West Saxon Kings, its bishop was a most powerful figure, holding the second richest diocese in the whole of Christendom (after Milan), and his Manor of Farnham was an important place.

It is important to remember that Domesday's reference to Farnham relates to the manor and not to the town. Although there is evidence that the settlement at what was to become the town of Farnham had a Saxon church, there is nothing to show that anything more than a few humble dwellings lay around it in Saxon times. Indeed, Tilford and Farnham might lay claim to similar status over many centuries. Tilford had the advantage of being at the confluence of two productive rivers whilst Farnham profited from its direct communications with London and Winchester. As the latter became increasingly important, Farnham acquired a castle and steadily grew in size and stature whilst Tilford continued as a village.

The Domesday Inquest gives a number of details for Farnham Manor. It speaks of a church - which was possibly on the site of the present day St Andrew's in Farnham but could have been a Saxon foundation elsewhere such as Frensham - and inhabitants comprising 78 tenants and their

> TERRA EPI WINTONIENSIS.
>
> .III. Eps Wintoniensis ten FERNEHAM. Scs petrvs
> sep tenuit. T.R.E. se defd p. LX. hid. 7 modo p. XL. hid.
> Tra. e.   In dnio sunt. v. car. 7 xxxvi. uilli 7 xi.
> bord cu. xxix. car. Ibi. xi. serui. 7 vi. molini de xlvi. solid
> 7 iiii. denar. 7 xxxv. ac pti. Silua: de. cl. porc. 7 dim̄ pasnag.
> De tra huj M ten de epo Radulf. iiii. hid una v min.
> Wills. iii. hid. Wazo. dimid hid. In his tris. iii. car in dnio.
> 7 xxii. uilli 7 ix. bord cu. vi. car. Silua: xxv. porc.
> T.R.E. ualb M. lv. lib qd jacet in Sudrie. Qdo recep: xxx.
> lib. Modo dniu epi: xxxviii. lib. Hominu ej: ix. lib.
> Æcclam huj M ten de epo Osbn de ow. Val. vi. lib. cu. i. hida
> qua ht in Hantesira.

15. Extract from the Surrey Domesday Survey A.D. 1086
(showing entry for the Bishop of Winchester's landholding)
(reproduced by kind permission from the Phillimore edition of DOMESDAY BOOK - General Editor John Morris - volume 3 Surrey, published in 1975 by Phillimore & Co Ltd, Shopwyke Manor Barn, Chichester, West Sussex, PO20 6BG.)

families and 11 slaves or serfs. These figures translate to a total population for the Manor of under 400 which is a density of around ten people per square mile. Clearly these would not have been spread out equally over the whole of the Manor but would have been concentrated in particular places. Looking at the map we can perhaps guess which localities might have been the likely settlements - these total some 20 places. The number of teams of ploughs in the manor according to Domesday was 43 which could be allocated to the 20 places to give a sensible distribution. Domesday also tells us that there were 6 mills and it has been suggested that these mills were at Elstead and Farnham (Bourne, Willey, Weydon, High, Hatch). However, this remains uncertain and, indeed, there may have been other mills elsewhere which were missed out by the Domesday surveyors.

What can be deduced about Tilford from these observations? Although no Farnham Manor villages are referred to in the Domesday Survey, Tilford is mentioned by name in the Waverley Abbey Charter of 1147 which confirms that by then, at least, it was a recognised place. Its favourable position alongside the junction of two rivers and reasonable distance from the London to Winchester road together with archaeological evidence from earlier times argues strongly for it being a well-established village at the time of Domesday. We can apportion two or three plough teams to the settlement, and using our earlier estimates of population, suggest there were some twenty five villagers. Although Tilford possessed it own mills later on, we cannot assume it had one in 1086, leaving corn to be carried elsewhere for milling.

The Domesday Inquest gave William vital information on the ability of his kingdom to pay tax and accordingly the land was assessed in *five-hide* units that bore little relation to actual area. Farnham Manor, previously assessed at *60 hides*, was reduced in value to *40 hides* by the Domesday Surveyors. Similarly, its value assessed in 1086 was said to be £53, whereas when acquired by William it was £30, and under Edward the Confessor it was £55. The sharp fall in value that took place between the time of Edward and William when he acquired it has been attributed to the devastation wrought on the land as William marched through it on his victorious campaign following 1066.

Based on this means of analysis, the line of William's advance can be seen to be a circuitous march round London passing through Guildford and Farnham to reach Winchester before returning northwards to cross the Thames at Wallingford in Berkshire and eventually to London. It is most likely that William's army would have travelled along the Hog's Back to reach Farnham from Guildford, with his troops pillaging the land over a wide area along the route. It is fanciful to think that in passing through Farnham, the troops would have violated Tilford but it seem more likely that the settlement would have been by-passed. Many of the Farnham inhabitants would have fled southwards in advance of the marauding Norman troops and the impact on the settlement at Tilford would have been both dramatic and frightening. With the army's departure to London, however, the inhabitants would have been able to return to resume their daily grind - shortly to work for a Norman master in Winchester in place of the Saxon landlord who had ruled their lives for so many years previously.

For the next 62 years the settlements at Farnham and Tilford continued to develop under the successive bishops of Winchester and no major incidents

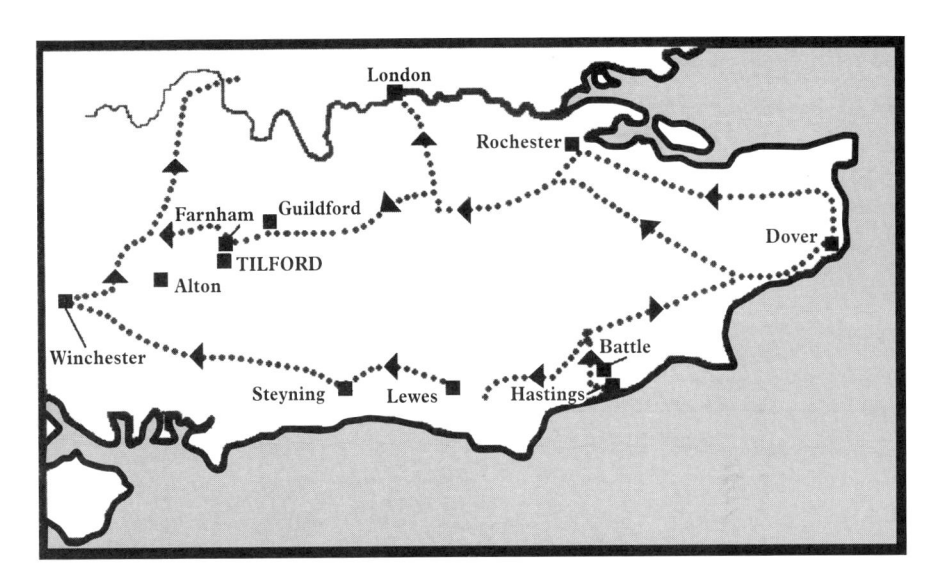

16. Line of William the Conqueror's March in 1066
(traced by using reduced values of manors in Domesday Book)

After landing at Hastings and defeating the Saxons at Battle, William advanced via Westerham and Bletchingley to Lewisham and Camberwell to a camp in Battersea before marching to Mortlake and Walton-on-Thames. There he struck south to Guildford and Farnham. Another part of William's army proceeded westwards along the South Downs before meeting up with the northern forces and making for Winchester.

interrupted the flow of most peoples' lives. In 1128, however, an event was to occur which had a fundamental impact on them and in particular on the inhabitants of Tilford. In that year William Giffard, the then bishop of Winchester, invited a group of twelve Cistercian monks and their Abbot from their Abbey at L'Aumone in Normandy to found a new community in his manor at Farnham. The site he chose was the land at Waverley along the river Wey between the settlements at Farnham and Tilford.

The reasons behind Giffard's choice of Farnham Manor remain unclear. He was an amiable character who tried to lead by example the monks at the Benedictine Abbey in Winchester away from their notorious fractious and insubordinate behaviour. Perhaps he wished to found a more disciplined community near at hand; or perhaps he felt that Caedwalla's gift of the Manor to the Christian community to found a *monasterium* had

35

not been properly fulfilled. Whatever the reason, he gave the Cistercians the 60 acres of land at Waverley, tithe free, to 'live freely and in peace for ever'; a beautiful and pious hope only partially to be fulfilled.

The Cistercian Order required the monks' community to be 'in places remote from the conversation of men' and not to be built 'in cities, in castles or villages'. It also had to be near a river. In Waverley, which must, at that time, have been uninhabited, they found an ideal place with a clear, deep stream, running through a valley in a secluded and protected spot.

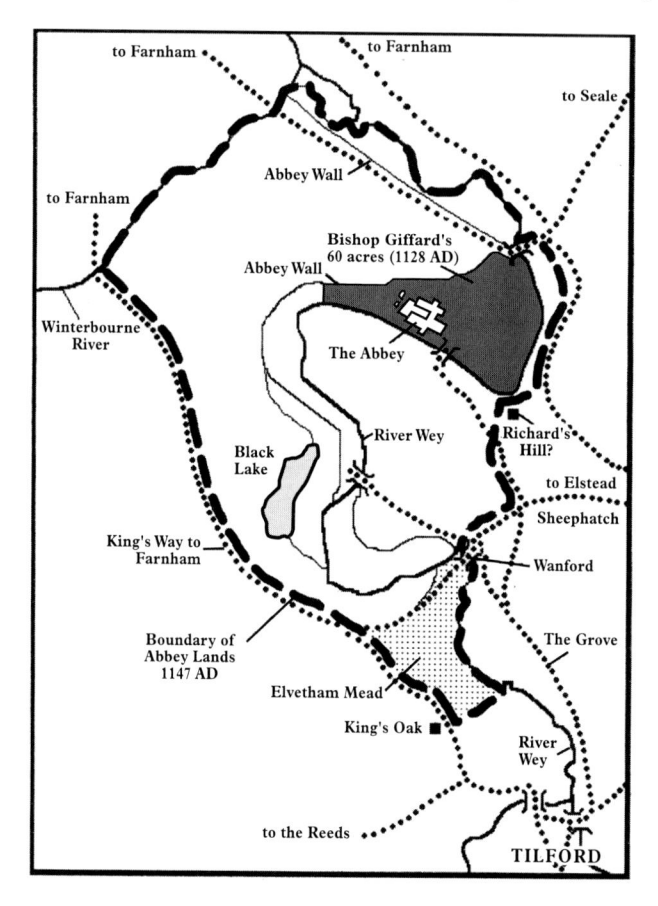

17. The Lands of Waverley Abbey

Founded in A.D. 1128 with a gift of sixty acres from Bishop Giffard of Winchester, Waverley Abbey grew to cover 540 acres by 1147.

There was clearly much work to do - clearing the forest, cultivating the land and erecting temporary shelters whilst they commenced their building work - but they were dedicated men and overcame their many obstacles with determination and a success for which the remains of their once magnificent Abbey stand in mute testimony.

William Giffard died only a very short time after the Abbey's foundation and was succeeded by King Steven's brother, Henry de Blois. It was he who built the first castle in Farnham - most probably a wooden one - some time before 1138; and it was he also who, nine years later, added to his predecessor's gift to the monks an additional virgate of land at Wanford. The so-called 'Liberty' of Henry, which authorised his gift, is interesting not only because of its intrinsic worth but chiefly because it defines the extent of the Abbey lands. It also includes the first mention of Tilford. The definition of the Abby's boundaries expressed in the 'Liberty' reads, in translation, as follows:

> "From the oak at Tileford called the Kynghoc by the King's way towards Farnham as far as the Wynterburn, and thence by its bank which runs from Farnham to the hill called Richardishulle and across the said hill and bridge at Waneford to the meadow of Tyleford called Ilvethammesmead and thence direct to the aforesaid oak."

The places mentioned in the 'Liberty' have been identified in different ways by many authors in the past. The area within this boundary is some 540 acres, far greater than the 60 acres awarded to the monks by Bishop Giffard and shows that there must have been a considerable encroachment of land over the 9 years since the Abbey's foundation. In effect, Henry de Blois' 'Liberty' sanctioned this increase and formalised the Abbey's new boundaries.

A common mistake made by some commentators has been to identify the 'Kynghoc' or King's Oak in the 'Liberty' with the famous King's Oak on Tilford Green, and 'Richardishulle' or Richard's Hill with Crooksbury Hill. Examination of later documents and of geographical limitations reveals that both these assumptions must be false. 'Ilvethammesmead' can be translated as 'the meadow of the swans at the bend of the river' and the 'Wynterburn' is the Bourne stream which, presumably, became significant only in the winter months. It is noteworthy that between Tilford and

Farnham there was at this date a recognised 'King's way' and that a bridge existed at Wanford (which can be translated as 'wagon ford').

18. Depiction of Waverley Abbey in the 14th Century
(reproduced by kind permission of English Heritige, 23 Savile Row, London, W1X 1AB)

The picture shows a view of the Abbey looking south. The great Abbey church is in the foreground and the river Wey can be seen in the distance.

The impact of Waverley Abbey on the budding town of Farnham and the village of Tilford must have been considerable. The community flourished and attracted many postulants. By 1187, numbers had swelled to 70 monks and 120 lay brothers and the great building work was well under way with around 30 plough teams at work on the estate. The Abbey buildings provided an ideal stopping place close to Farnham for travellers between London and Winchester and attracted the King and his Court on their customary moves between these two cities. As Etienne Robo remarks in his book on Waverley Abbey (first published in 1935):

"The Angevin Kings were found more often on the road than in their palace at Westminster. The Court, always travelling, was like a town on the move; soldiers, courtiers, clerks, councillors, executioners, judges with their clerks, plaintiffs and defendants waiting for judgement, exchequer officials with their accounts and their bullion stored in little wooden barrels, a host of servants and followers, accompanied the King wherever he went."

Such a horde stopping at Farnham would have encouraged expansion and trade. During the civil war between Stephen and Matilda, Henry de Blois had raised a shell keep of stone round the mound of Farnham Castle and the town was fast becoming a place of importance for both church and crown. On the opposite side of Waverley to Farnham, Tilford would have reaped many benefits from the increasing importance and prosperity of the abbey and the town. There would have been opportunities for employment on the abbey lands, the abbey's apothecary and herbalist would have been available for medical advice, and some trade in goods must have taken place between the villagers and the community. The monks, as ordained priests, would have travelled around the villages celebrating mass and dispensing the sacraments, whilst the lay brothers would have had contact with the locals through their management of agriculture, particularly sheep farming. A fictitious account of relations between the monks of Waverley and the people of Tilford has been drawn up by Arthur Conan Doyle in his book 'Sir Nigel' (first published in 1906) which, although inaccurate in detail and from a later period, conveys a sense of the atmosphere that would have existed in the Abbey's hey-days.

The Cistercians were famous for their agricultural expertise and the Order in England became pre-eminent in sheep farming; and at Waverley much of the land must have been given over to grazing for the Abbey's flocks of sheep which, it has been estimated, must have run into thousands. At the boundary between Waverley and Tilford is Sheephatch which name would indicate that there was some form of hatch or gate at this point for the sheep to pass through. Such sheep may well have been driven down into Tilford for additional grazing, and indeed it is likely that the two bridges over the Wey at Tilford Green may well have been built by the monks for the purpose of enabling the flocks to get across to the south side of the river; certainly, later on, we have evidence that land there was rented by them for such grazing.

These two bridges were, it is believed, originally made of wood but were rebuilt in stone probably after the disastrous floods of 1233 during which water levels rose by eight feet 'destroying and overturning bridges, walls and ways'. The builder is thought to have been Brother John of Waverley who by 1226 was of sufficient standing as a mason to undertake royal contracts and who is believed to have designed and built the whole series of stone bridges across the Wey from Farnham to Guildford. These bridges remain today as a testimony to the craftsmanship of their creator; they are recognised landmarks in Tilford and are listed as ancient monuments.

19. Tilford's East Bridge

Tilford's two mediaeval stone bridges were constructed by the monks of Waverley Abbey in the 13th century and are still in continuous use today.

In addition to their bridges, the monks also built a number of water mills, two of which were in what is now Tilford. One of these was erected at Wanford (Tilford Mill) and the other just outside the Abbey itself (Waverley Mill). They continued in operation until well into the nineteenth century. Later on, fish ponds were constructed to meet the changing eating-habits of the monks; two of these, Abbot's Pond and Black Lake, were created in Tilford. The former lasted until 1841 whilst the latter still remains intact. The bridges, water mills and ponds constructed by the monks all had their impact on Tilford, and as will be seen later on, were important factors in the village's development.

Chapter 7

Mediaeval Tilford

As we move through the mediaeval period, the records of the Bishop of Winchester, the Lord of the Manor of Farnham, become increasingly more extensive and useful. As we have seen in the previous chapter, the Bishop of Winchester was a very powerful figure of immense wealth whose estates spread over six of today's counties. It was he who owned the land and he who exercised judicial authority. Most of the inhabitants of Farnham Manor were bondmen, that is they had been born in the hundred and were bound to stay within it, leasing and renting land from the bishop and paying him taxes. Certain men had bought their freedom from bondage and there were a few others who had settled in the manor as freemen. In the town of Farnham, which had achieved the status of borough in the 12th century, the inhabitants had obtained at an early date and in exchange for a yearly payment, a large amount of self-government. Waverley Abbey was, of course, by its charter, *extra parochial* and the monks held the land freehold, a fact that was to become increasingly significant later on after the dissolution.

In Tilford none of these dispensations from bondage applied, and right up to modern times, land was held from the bishop through copyhold. Whenever copyhold land passed from one person to another, either by inheritance or through sale, a *fine* was levied to the bishop indicating, as the Latin word implies, an end to the tenancy. Such transfers had to be approved by the bishop but as he generally was anxious to obtain rent without delay, they were rarely, if ever, obstructed. The bishop's clerks kept meticulous records of these transfers and the bishop's *fine* entries are a great source of information for the historian. In addition to this, the bishop's court rolls and pipe rolls (so called because at one time pipes were used for storage) give valuable facts and figures concerning the bishop's financial accounts, the administration of his estates and the imposition of justice.

Unfortunately, the very large number of these documents and the language in which they are written have proved obstacles to their publication and to date, only two years of the pipe rolls for the whole of the bishop's estates (those for 1301-2 and 1409-10) have so far been made available in translation. However, a limited number of selected pipe roll records for Farnham Manor from the thirteenth century until the seventeenth have been translated, notably by Philip Brooks of Churt; and these enable us to get some idea of who lived in Tilford over that time and the conditions under which they earned their living. The everyday life of the people of Farnham Manor has been admirably described in 'Mediaeval Farnham', written by Etienne Robo and published in the mid-1930's, and will not be repeated here. However, the records can be investigated specifically for Tilford and with the background information provided by Robo and others, we can create a feeling for life in the village in mediaeval times.

At the start of the period, in the first half of the 13th century, very few of the bishop's tenants possessed a real surname common to all the members of the same family. They were mostly known by their Christian names. However, for more precision they were referred to by their parentage (such as Richard son of Robert), by their trade (such as Thomas the Tiler), or by their place of living (such as of the Hatch or at the Stone). This provides useful information and we can get some idea of the trades and locations of people by reference to the records of their names.

Many of the names and titles listed for Tilford can be interpreted easily; for example: Wydemed (or 'Widemead' ie wide meadow) is present-day Whitmead; Wodehulle is Woodhill; Crokesburwe is Crooksbury; and 'Tileford' and 'Tillehulle' are some of the many variants of Tilford and Tilhill. The trades and other descriptions of the Tilford villagers are sometimes more difficult to translate. 'Fisher', 'Mower', 'Newman', 'Smith' and 'Brewer' are self-evident and those relating to the cloth trade such as 'Fuller', 'Kember' (or Comber), 'Webbe(r)' and 'Tenter' (or Stretcher), are readily interpreted. However, some of the other names are obscure and more research needs to be done in this area before full identification of all the trades is possible.

As bondmen, the villagers of Tilford had their lives strictly controlled by the bishop. Licences were required for most actions: for marriage, for example, and for sub-letting land. In addition, the bondmen were required to work on the bishop's own farms. Rather like planning controls today, there were strict rules governing 'disturbance of the soil' and fines were enacted for house-building and demolition; even to dig a ditch, a licence had to be obtained from the bishop. Such rules and regulations governing the lives of the men and women of Tilford may not be totally dissimilar to those of today but in their quality of life, there can be no comparison.

Lack of machinery and fertilisers led to devastatingly poor returns from the land and with difficulty of transport restricting commerce and access, the villagers were hard put to meet the burden of rent, taxes and other fees due to the bishop and king, let alone have any spare capital for investment. Although there were those very few who were able to save enough to purchase their 'liberty', this did not happen very often.

In next-door Waverley Abbey, the monks had become firmly established by the start of the 13th century and in 1203 they started to build their magnificent Abbey Church. No sooner, however, were the foundations dug than they were forced to disperse by a 'great famine and the dying of men' which compelled them to seek asylum in other religious houses. The cause of this disaster was undoubtedly a failure of the harvest and the villagers of Tilford would have suffered a similar fate. The river Wey was at this time subject to frequent floods and the Waverley Annals record that in 1201, for example, 'buildings were inundated and great damage done to the crops'.

Tilford farmers, in eking out a bare living, had much to contend with from nature; but it wasn't only nature that dealt them dire blows. In 1216 the relative peace of the countryside was shattered by Louis the Dauphin when the French army occupied Farnham Castle. Following the offer by the English barons of the English crown to Philip of France, Louis landed at Sandwich on May 30th 1216. King John, whose crown was thus in jeopardy, marched in haste to Winchester with Louis in pursuit, taking Reigate on Tuesday June 18th, Guildford on Wednesday, and Farnham Castle on Friday.

The French occupation lasted nearly a year and in the pipe rolls we have evidence of the damage the French army inflicted on the countryside. There are reports of 'wheat, oats and barley plundered', of 'sheep, pigs and horses stolen' and 'wethers, hoggs and cheeses taken'; one of the bishop's mills was damaged and many repairs to buildings had to be undertaken. Much of the corn was 'wasted' and commerce and the passage of goods was interrupted. This, combined with the disruption in the normal planting schedule and breeding programme of the local farmers and the necessity of continuing to meet the bishop's demands for payment of rent, had very serious consequences for Tilford and it would be some 30 or 40 years before it completely recovered from the French invasion.

Waverley Abbey was, however, apparently little affected and continued to grow in stature and importance. With their emphasis on agriculture, the Cistercians relied heavily on the recruitment of laymen for their survival and Tilford would have provided easy access to the local labour market. Sheep farming was predominant and by the middle of the 13th century the export of wool by the English Cistercians had become a feature in the commerce of the country. With the manufacture of woollen cloth forming the staple industry of this part of west Surrey, and a range of fulling mills at the disposal of the monks, sheep farming and its associated work would have been a major activity for the villagers in Tilford.

The names of Tilford's principal land holdings are maintained in the records over many centuries and it is possible by careful analysis to determine to which areas the names refer. These areas are the bond-lands granted to the tenants by the Lord of the Manor. Whilst ownership changed, the pattern of landholding remained very much the same - right down until recent times. In all, twenty different names of 'plots' have been identified. Most of the plots have names that go back to the earliest records but for three land holdings (*viz* Chapel Farm, Squires Hill Farm and Tilford House Farm) no 'ancient' names have been discovered and modern day titles have been used in any reference to them. Some titles such as 'Ketts', 'Sturt', 'Birchin Reeds' *etc* are of later date. In addition to the Tilford plots, there is the virgate at Wanford which was included in Tilford later on. This virgate was part of Waverley Abbey lands until 1654 when it was sold freehold to Robert Palmer who was the miller at Tilford Mill. Finally, there is 'Elthams' which is thought to describe the rod ($1/4$ acre) of bond-land of the island in the river Wey on which John Elvetham constructed his fulling mill and which later, because of changes in the course of the river, became part of the bank.

The origin of the bond-lands is obscure, dating back possibly to Saxon or even Roman times. Each bondman was allotted an area measured in 'half-virgates' which was originally the amount of land an ox could plough in a year. This, of course, depended on the quality of the soil and hence varied across the country. In Surrey, a virgate was normally taken to be 30 acres.

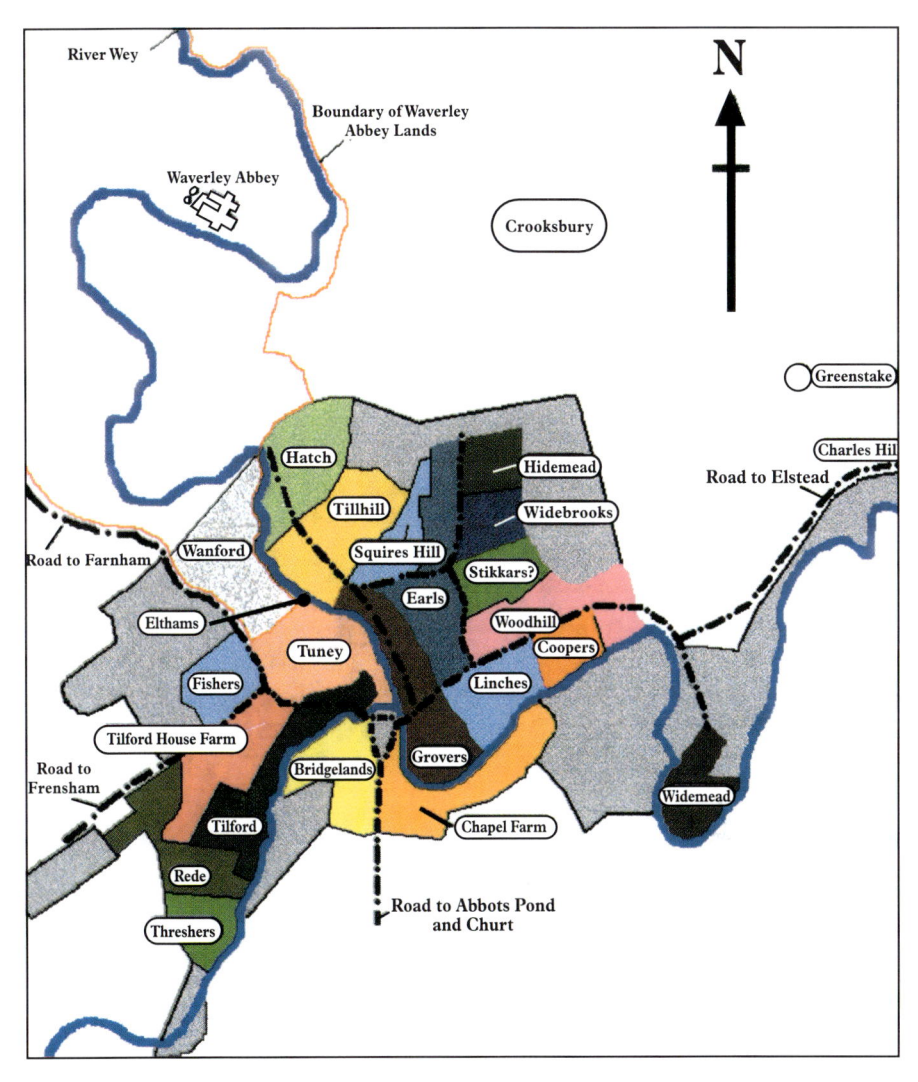

20. Tilford's Bond Lands

Tilford's bond lands were properties - normally either ¹/₂ Virgate (15 acres) or one virgate (30 acres) in size - on which the Lord of the Manor (the Bishop of Winchester) claimed feudal service. The village of Tilford was composed of 20 bond holdings covering 15 ¹/₂ virgates; these are labelled on the diagram and shown in colour (Wanford was part of Waverley Abbey). Seventeen of these have 'ancient' names; for the remaining three (Tilford House Farm, Chapel Farm, and Squires Hill Farm) no early names have been found. The unnamed areas in the diagram shaded in grey indicate land taken in from the waste in mediaeval times.

By 1332, some farms in Tilford had doubled in size to 1 virgate; one ('Earls') was $2^1/_2$ half-virgates, and one ('Coopers') was only $^1/_2$ a half-virgate. The bondman's obligations to the Lord of the Manor was based on his bondland holding but he could also hold land that he had taken in from the 'waste'. This was called 'purpresture' land. In good times, more and more 'waste' land was cultivated, and this brought in more income both to the farmer and to the bishop who exacted rent both on bond land and on purpresture land.

Other than the splitting up of some of the virgate holdings (*eg* 'Tilford') back into half-virgates and the amalgamation of others (*eg* 'Grovers' with 'Stikkars'), the bond-land holdings remained broadly the same until recent times. However, the total area under cultivation varied markedly because of, on the one hand, purpresture land being taken in from the waste and, on the other, a dereliction of land from natural causes.

Apart from Bridgeland and 'Chapel Farm', the farming community was confined to the land on the north of the river where much of the alluvial deposits was concentrated. Moreover, until the monks of Waverley Abbey bridges had constructed the bridges across the river, it would have been more convenient working in the northern part of the settlement. The area of the bond-lands in Tilford amounted to $15^1/_2$ virgates (or 465 acres) and we can estimate that, in addition, land taken in from the waste by the mid 14th century amounted to some 60 acres. Thus the total area under cultivation at this time was of the order of some 525 acres, or about a fifth of the total area of modern-day Tilford.

To the south of the river, was the bishop's warren where game such as pheasant, partridge, fox, rabbit, hare, and other small animals could be hunted. At this time rabbits, which were Mediterranean animals that had been introduced into England by the Normans, were highly sensitive and burrowing had to be encouraged by the building of special earth works. The warrens, which yielded much prized meat and fur, were a valuable facility and strongly protected. In 1250, the bishop gave the monks of Waverley Abbey part of his warren "from a little bridge [ie stock bridge] below Tilleford along the watercourse, which is called Crikeledburne, towards Cherte" at an annual rent of 6s.8d to enable them to construct a fish pond. This was finished a year later and became known as 'Abbot's Pond'.

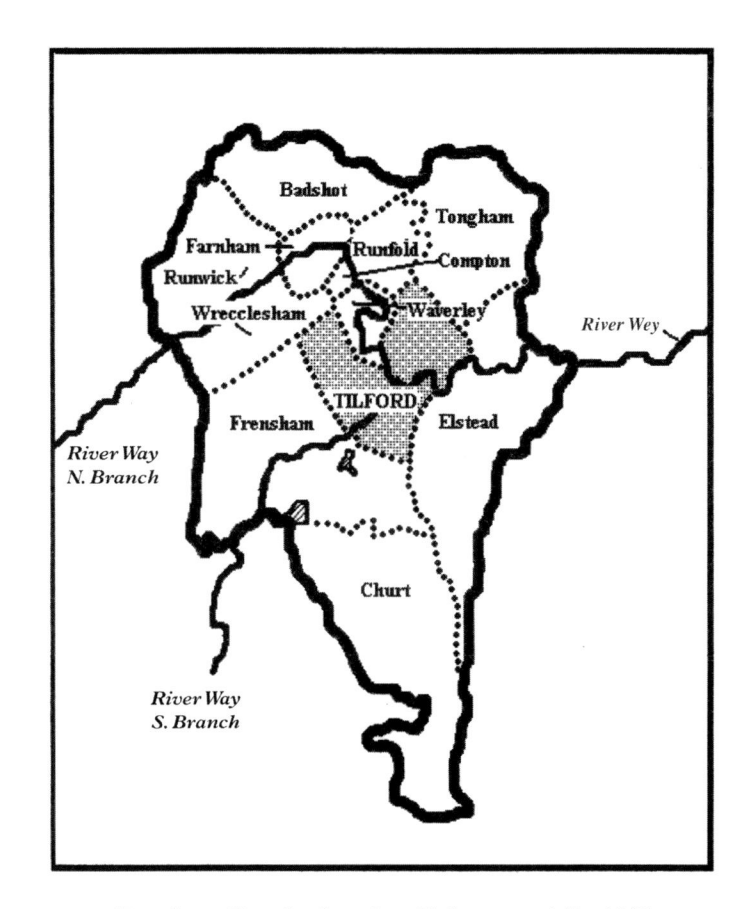

21. Farnham Hundred and its Tithings ~ A.D. 1332

For administrative and tax purposes, Farnham Manor was treated as a 'Hundred' and divided into 'Tithings'. As the name implies, there should be ten tithings and the diagram shows those identified in the tax records (Surrey Lay Subsidies) of A.D.1332. Additional tithings' names, such as 'Dogflud', 'Culverland', 'Seale', and 'Bourn', have appeared in the records at other times.

The erection of two of the abbey's fulling mills in present-day Tilford - one at Wanford and the other by the bridge at Waverley - was noted in the previous chapter. In 1338, a certain John Elvetham paid the bishop 3s. 4d for 'an island in the middle of the river at Tilford 5 perches by 1 perch [ie 80 feet x 16 feet] to erect a fulling mill, with easement for the use of water.' It is not exactly clear where this island was but a number of leads point to a position where the boundary of Wanford meets that of Tilford and which was subsequently named 'Elthams'. Sadly, Elvetham's initiative did not last for long for, in 1366, the bishop's clerks record that William at the Hatch paid 2 shillings for 'land at Tilford where the fulling mill used to be'.

In addition to the Bishop of Winchester's records, there were those of the crown. We have already seen how the Domesday Inquest in 1086 produced a unique record. Such assessments, made inevitably for the levying of tax, continued without ceasing. Between 1290 and 1332 sixteen grants or subsidies were levied by the monarchs as methods of raising revenue. The records of many of these have not survived but Surrey is fortunate in having a comprehensive set for the whole county for the year 1332. The tax was levied on a 'hundred' which, in turn, was divided into 'tithings'. Tilford comprised one tithing of Farnham Hundred; others included Elstead, Tongham, Frensham, Churt, and those surrounding the town of Farnham.

Whereas the bishop's records can be used to identify changes in the details of individuals over time, the tax data give a 'snap-shot' in time of the village as a whole. By combining the two it becomes possible to identify names and relationships and associate people with their properties. Unfortunately, the records do not generally give descriptions of these properties in sufficient detail to identify their locations accurately and this, combined with breaks in continuity and the difficulties of translation and interpretation, makes tracking such associations down the centuries much more of an art than a science. Many assumptions and inferences have to be made and the end result can be open to different interpretations.

An attempt has been made, using all the records available, to link the people of Tilford with the known land holdings. After allowing for the anomalies, comparison of the bishop's records with the tax records of 1332, makes it possible to estimate the population of Tilford in that year. Twenty six principal tenants can be identified and we can deduce a further six cottagers making a total, in all, of 32 families. To convert these to individuals, it is necessary to multiply by a factor representing the average number of people per family. This leads to a figure for the Tilford population in 1332 of around 135 and is the first reasonably reliable assessment of numbers in the village since the time of the Domesday survey.

The picture of early 14th century Tilford that emerges is of a small self-contained farming community containing within its ranks a number of tradesmen who worked for the abbey such as the fuller, the comber and the tenter who were employed at one or other of the village's fulling mills, the fishermen who worked one or more of the village's three fisheries or 'weirs' on the Wey, and the weavers who worked at home on their looms.

It is not possible from the data to assess the uses to which the land was being put but we know that, for the Manor as a whole, the crops consisted of wheat, barley and oats, with animals comprising cart-horses, plough-horses, oxen, bullocks, sheep, pigs and hens, and Tilford would have had a similar pattern.

In 1301, the bishop's clerks recorded the production of ale and bread, eggs, butter and ewe's and cow's cheese; also recorded were wool fleeces, lamb's wool, woolskins, bare skins and lambskins. Whilst the clerks made no records of honey production at Tilford, we know that bee-keeping was a very important industry in England from Roman times and honey was mentioned specifically in one of the early charters of Farnham Manor. The heathland around Tilford would have been an ideal foraging ground for the bees and honey, as the villagers' sole access to sugar, must be assumed to have strongly featured in their diet. Fish, either directly caught from the river or purchased in Farnham or from the Abbey, would have been an occasional treat as an alternative to the rare occasions when meat was available.

Towards the end of the 13th century, there was an increase in the land under cultivation, which would indicate a growth in the economy - but there was little sign of increased prosperity. Each year the villagers had to rely on the quality of the harvest, which sometimes failed them disastrously, and had to cope with the regular flooding of the Wey that was often very destructive. On top of this, animal diseases afflicted their livestock and sometimes threatened their very survival. Nothing, however, had prepared them for the greatest calamity yet which was to hit them in the middle of the next century and which was going to completely disrupt and revolutionise their way of life and almost wipe out their village. This, the Black Death, hit the south of England in 1348.

By the end of 1346 it was widely known in European seaports that a plague of unparalleled fury was raging in the east but none thought this would be the harbinger of what was soon to hit nearer home. Over the next five years the 'great pestilence' swept across Europe destroying, it is estimated, a quarter of its inhabitants. The bubonic plague, known as the Black Death on account of the appearance of its victims, reached England in the summer of 1348 probably through Melcombe Regis in Dorset. By October the plague was rife in many parts of Dorset and by the end of the year it had reached Farnham Manor. In his book on Mediaeval Farnham, Robo contends that Tongham and Tilford were the first villages in the Manor to suffer, but later writers have challenged this.

Whatever the case, the effect on Tilford was catastrophic with over half the farms losing their heads of household in the first year. Of the twenty-four principal tenants in Tilford in 1348, only one can be declared a certain survivor. Of the remaining twenty-three, eighteen had given up their tenancies by 1351 and three had defaulted completely on paying their rents. Although we can't be sure that all these died as a result of the Black Death, it is likely that the majority succumbed to the ravages of the successive waves of the plague which extended from 1348 to 1351 - a shocking twenty-one heads of household out of twenty-four total.

The cottagers are likely to have suffered in the same way although the records are not so clear-cut as are those for the principal tenants. Of the ten cottage tenancies listed in 1348, two tenants are known to have given up their holdings during the plague years and a third was unable to pay any rent. It must be assumed that these three were also victims of the plague; (of the seven others noted in 1332, the records for four of them in 1348 are missing). Overall, therefore, at least 24 out of 34 or some 70%, of Tilford's heads of households are likely to have perished in the Black Death and the total may well have been much higher.

It is impossible to estimate how many members of the tenants' families also fell victim to the disease. In some cases, the wife, son or daughter took on the tenancy indicating that, in these cases, the first victims of the plague were limited to the husband. However, the widows themselves often succumbed in the following year. Eventually, it was often an outsider who came in and took over or, as was the case in many others, the farm was left untenanted.

In the manor as a whole it has been estimated that, over the three years of the Black Death, the plague resulted in the deaths of more than a third of the inhabitants. It is notable, however, that Tilford was hit disproportionately compared with elsewhere. Over the three years of the plague years, whilst the whole of the manor had 123 defaults of rent, in Tilford there were 29 - some quarter of the total. Considering that the population of the village was only some 5 to 10% of that of the Manor, it can readily be seen how badly Tilford suffered relative to elsewhere.

Paradoxically, the bishop initially gained from the income generated by the increased level of *fines* resulting from the transfer of property on death, but it was not long before this was far outweighed by the reduction in rent income from those unable to pay. For a hundred years or more after 1348, many of the farms in the manor were abandoned or derelict and year after year until around 1500, the bishop's pipe rolls for Tilford record continuing defaults of rent.

It was a sorry landscape that faced those in the village who had survived the plague (which was to revisit the manor again in 1361) and who were now barely able to make any sort of living let alone pay the rent. Land was being left idle and houses and mills were decaying. Such devastation combined with a weak national economy resulting from the incessant wars of the 15th century, left Tilford in a state of depressed poverty for a century and a half. Eventually, with the arrival of the Tudors, the economy began to improve, the village's desolate and often deserted lands started to yield profits, houses of more substantial structure were built on the run-down tofts, and 'defaults of rent' finally became a thing of the past.

As we pass out of the Middle Ages, Tilford begins to take up its modern form. The farmlands whose names and shapes we have recognised in the mediaeval period have been retained and extended, and it becomes possible, using the records, to determine the development of each one individually. The low point in Tilford's history is over and we come to the Tudors and await the appearance of Henry VIII in 1509 and the next major event in the story of the village, the dissolution of Waverley Abbey.

Chapter 8

Tudor Times

The accession of Henry VII to the throne of England in 1485 brought in the Tudor dynasty and the start of the modern period of British history. Tilford had emerged from the passivity of the Middle Ages into a world of Renaissance and change, of exploration and adventure, and at a local level, the abandonment of the rigid rules of peasant allegiance to the Lord of the Manor. Not that taxes, rents, and other levies were any less burdensome, but the Black Death and its aftermath had led to serious labour shortages, and economic pressures had forced many of the old restrictions to disappear. As the Tudor period advanced, there were more opportunities for the acquisition of wealth and more substantial houses started to be built in consequence of rising prosperity among the smaller number of land-holders. Early on, the period was marked with the dissolution of the monasteries under Henry VIII and many see this as the real end of the mediaeval era.

Waverley Abbey was one of the first monasteries to fall, and its demise in 1536 effected a break in a continuity that had lasted for over 400 years and must have been a shock to the villagers of Tilford who had been brought up believing that the *status quo* was immutable. In practical terms, however, the impact was muted. At the time of the dissolution, numbers in the Abbey had dwindled to only a very few monks and their disappearance would not have been as traumatic as it would have been in previous times when the Abbey would have housed several hundred monks and lay brothers. Nevertheless, the vacuum created by their evacuation at the behest of Thomas Cromwell, Henry's Chancellor, would not have been without its consequences on the village. Barter and trade between the villagers and the lay brothers at the abbey would have come to an abrupt end and those in the village who were employed at the abbey would have been fearful and uncertain whether they would be re-hired. The more enterprising would, of course, have looked out for new openings and it would be surprising if local negotiations over the disposition of the abbey's farm animals and goods before the new owner of Waverley took over had not lead to a few profitable deals for Tilford's farmers.

*22. Portrait of Fitzwilliam,
Earl of Southampton
By Hans Holbein Jnr*

(reproduced by kind permission of the Surrey Archaeological Society, Castle Arch, Guildford, GU1 3SX.)

Sir William Fitzwilliam was Lord High Admiral of England, Knight of the Garter, and Treasurer of the King's Household when King Henry VIII granted Waverley Abbey to him in July 1537. In October of the same year, he was raised to the peerage as Earl of Southampton.

The new owner chosen by Henry VIII for Waverley was Sir William Fitzwilliam, Knight of the Garter, and Treasurer of the King's Household. What Fitwilliam felt about gaining the abbey is not recorded but as it provided an income of less than £200 a year, and as he already had large estates at Cowdray and in Hampshire, it is likely he took it over without great enthusiasm. Everything worth selling was sold - chalices, vestments, banners, books and anything else that could be carried away. Of great material value was the lead of the roof and at the base of the columns. These were dismantled and the benches and stalls of the church were burned to provide the fires for the lead to be melted. The resulting devastation left the abbey open to the ravages of wind and weather and initiated a prolonged period of destruction.

On Fitzwilliam's death in 1542, the Cowdray estate and Waverley fell to his half-brother Sir Anthony Browne. It is ironic that Sir Anthony was a staunch Roman Catholic. His son, also Sir Anthony, inherited both his father's strong religious principles and on his father's death in 1549, Waverley Abbey. In 1554, on the occasion of Mary's marriage with Philip of Spain, he was created a viscount and chose the title of Montague. At this time, Waverley Abbey, in spite of its earlier deprivations, was still habitable and its previous links with Tilford remained. But further devastation was soon to occur. Montague was friends with Sir William More, the owner of Loseley House near Guildford and over the six years from 1562 to 1568, cartloads of stone were taken from Waverley to enable Sir William to rebuild his house - leaving the abbey buildings in a completely ruinous state.

The Tudor owners of Waverley were absentee landlords and took little or no direct part in the affairs of Tilford. However, their tenants had close connections. One of the best known of these was Benedict Jay, Queen Elizabeth's Woodsman, who held the Manor of Frensham Beale and was a well-known figure in Farnham. He rented land in Tilford to add to that which he farmed in Waverley itself. He was succeeded by his son Francis, followed by Richard Harding, and finally by William Pyke who was a suspected recusant and regarded in the district as something of a renegade. Upon Viscount Montague's death in 1592, Waverley passed to his grandson, the second Lord Montague, who sold it in 1609 to John Coldham.

In Tilford, as we have seen, the Black Death of 1348-51 had been devastating and it had taken a century and a half for the village to recover. During those intervening years however, particularly during the second half of the fifteenth century, much land had been reclaimed and the picture at the start of the sixteenth century mirrored that of earlier, more productive, times. Cultivated land extended all along the river and also at Crooksbury. Isolated cottages and their curtilages had been established along the road to Frensham (at Pierrepont Reeds and what is now the site of the Rural Life Centre) and close to Abbots Pond.

In the years following the Black Death, many land-holdings had become amalgamated either through marriage or by the take-over of vacant tenancies, and by 1500 there were many fewer tenants than in 1348. It was a very close-knit community, with landholders or their close relations owning other properties - both in Tilford and elsewhere in the manor.

Once again, as in 1332, we are fortunate in having an intact record of rent payers for the village at a critical time. This record is especially valuable as it was drawn up in 1530, before the Reformation, with an overlay of detail for 1570, after the Reformation. From this document we can deduce that in 1530 there were twelve (half as many) principal tenants holding the same number (15^1/$_2$) of virgates as in 1348; also, three of the tenants - the Hardings - were from the same family. The allocation of lands to these tenants is not immediately deducible but can be partially understood from the 'line of descent' of the property throughout the years.

23. Linches (Upper Street) Farm House, Tilford

Upper Street Farm House is one of Tilford's older houses dating from the 15th century. Constructed originally as an 'open hall house', it has been considerably altered and extended over the years. In 1568 the Bishop of Winchester fined Richard and Helen Novell £6.13s. 0d. for 'letting the house at Linches fall down'.

The increase in prosperity over the Tudor period gave rise to the construction of houses that were generally much more substantial than previously. There are at least eight houses in Tilford dating, at least in part, from this period that are still standing and occupied today. These are: Tilford Farmhouse (Bridge Cottage), Tilford House Farmhouse, Street Farmhouse, Upper Street Farmhouse, Malthouse, and Sheephatch Farmhouse together with Bridge Farmhouse and No 1 Tilford Green

Cottages. The first six correspond with the messuages belonging respectively to the Tilford, Tuney, Grovers, Linches, Bridgeland and Hatch virgates whilst the last two were on land specifically allocated for house-building. In addition to these six messuages, there were those belonging to the other principal tenants but these have not survived - either they were not so well-built or their owners, later on, decided to replace them rather than extend or renew them. Originally, all the half-virgates would have had their messuages, but in the fifteenth century after the Black Death, when the population dropped so catastrophically and many of the bondland farms amalgamated under new owners, those redundant to use would have been left to decay.

Outside of their work on the farms, the lives of the villagers in Tilford were circumscribed by religion and the law. Much has been written on the impact of the Reformation on people's attitudes to religious observance and social behaviour and a great deal of this is conflicting, tainted with the beliefs and prejudices of individual writers. In his book on Mediaeval Farnham, Etienne Robo devotes a chapter to the changes that occurred immediately after the Reformation. He notes that the dissolution of Waverley Abbey had little direct effect on the religious life of Farnham but that subsequent events produced highly significant changes. In 1547, for example, shortly after Henry VIII's death, Stephen Gardiner, the then Bishop of Winchester, was sent to Fleet Prison in London for finding fault with proposed new books on religious innovations and preaching, and many injunctions soon came into force ordering the dissolution of Farnham's Chantry school, the destruction of images and shrines, and the forbidding of processions and other religious customs. Farnham church, which the villagers of Tilford would have attended, was then one of the richest in this part of the country and many valuable furnishings and vestments were removed by the king's commissioners. A new Calvinist attitude to religious practice took hold, and by the time of Elizabeth I, 'witch-hunts' against Catholics had become rampant as the following petition of 1584 to Queen Elizabeth issued by Bishop Cooper (one of Gardiner's successors) illustrates:

> "That it may please you to give in charge to the sheriff and some of the most forward gentlemen, once in a month or three weeks upon the sudden to have a privy search in sundry suspected places, where it is thought Jesuits or seminary men have their recourse and refuge, to seduce her Majesty's subjects".

It was in response to this that a 'presentment' was made to the Bishop of Winchester concerning the conduct of William Pyke who has already been mentioned above. This presentment, dated 7th March 1591 and made for the town and parish of Farnham, reads as follows:

> "We (whose name are underwritten) do present that touching this presentment service for the inquiry after Jesuits, Seminaries, Recusants, and such like suspicious persons, there are none to be found in the said town and parish to our knowledge. But that there is an Abbey called Waverley, distant from Farnham a mile or thereabouts, wherein there dwelt some time Mr Benedict Jay, who with his household did usually come to the church of divine service at Farnham and received the sacrament there. Since his departure one Richard Harding dwelt in the said Abbey, and did likewise come to the said church to the divine service, and received the sacrament there with his family. Now of late years, one William Pyke is dwelling in the said Abbey who baptises and buries his people at Farnham Church aforesaid, notwithstanding neither the said William Pyke, nor his wife, nor his family, to our knowledge, for this three years past or thereabouts, hath come to the said church at Farnham to the divine service there on the Sabbath days, nor hath for himself or his wife received the sacraments of the Lord's Supper there as usually others have done before him, nor hath repaired to any other church to the divine service to our knowledge. Peter Hampden, John More, the mark of John Figg, William Welsh."

It is not known what action, if any, was ever taken against recusant Pyke. Peter Hampden was bailiff in Farnham and was believed to have lived in Tilford, and it was the same man who gave evidence in a dispute between Lord Montague and Sir George More over fishing rights in the Wey between Tancredsford and Waverley Abbey. In a letter to Sir George (as quoted by the Reverend R.N. Milford in his book on Farnham published in 1859) he says in rather quaint English and in what today would be described as a self-deprecating, sycophantic, manner:

> "Right worshipful, your pleasure is I should let you understand what I can say concerning the fishing of Waverley house in the great river. This is ever what I had to do with the river. They did challenge of the fishing from Tancredsford to Ceykin lake and so often times did

fish it; and this colour they have for it. Some time they had the post of the weir, some of them are yet standing as I think; and again they say they pay for the fishing, and a little house which stands upon Tilford side, 4d a year unto my Lord Bishop. And further, one Mills of Tilford, who was deputy under Jack Winkfield afore my time, told me they did fish it; which Mills was my deputy till your good father had to do with it. And this much is that I can say concerning it, I would to God it were in me to do your worship any service or pleasure, you should find me ready ever, upon my knees, to do it, for the kindness I found in that worshipful man your father and you always; and thus I end praying to the Almighty God to bless you in this world with all happiness, in the world to come endless joy. Your worship's poor and distressed friend, Peter Hampden. Ps I am ashamed of my boldness in writing to your worship, but I am a distressed old man upon whom please you to bestow your charity by the bearer. I shall ever pray for you."

'Ceytin lake' is presumably Frensham Little Pond, which used to be called 'Crowsfoot Pond' on ancient maps, and the 'little house which stands on the Tilford side' is perhaps where Chuter's cottage stands today.

There is no doubt that the village was kept in deference to authority - whether it was to the sovereign, the bishop, or the local member of the aristocracy. These three, between them, levied rents, rates and taxes and the administration of justice. In return, the villagers were able to exercise peacefully and benefit from the increasing prosperity of the country. A measure of relative wealth can be made by comparing the tax returns from the Elizabethan era with those of 1332. Such taxes were euphemistically termed 'Lay Subsidies' and were so-called to distinguish them from impositions on the clergy. A full set of records for Surrey is available for 1594 and from this it can be deduced that the rural communities of the manor fared badly compared with Farnham town. Of course, this may have reflected the greater ability of rural folk to disguise their assets but the difference is marked, with Tilford at the lower end of the scale contributing only $3^1/_2$ % of the total in 1594 compared with $6^1/_2$ % in 1332.

Such a reduction in relative wealth stemmed both from the general malaise of the fifteenth century as well as from the effects of the Black Death on numbers of people in employment on the farms. It has been suggested that there were fewer people in the whole of England in the sixteenth century than there were in 1300. In the case of Tilford, we have already noted that in 1530 and 1570 the number of bondland tenants in the village was only a half of those in 1348. On the other hand, we know that much land that had been taken in from the 'waste' needed cultivation and that people had settled in various isolated cottages in Crooksbury, Charles Hill, the Reeds, and near Abbots Pond. It is clear from other sources such as the records of assizes that Tilford was home to a broader range of families than just those of the principal tenants. For example, we learn that in 1569, Arnold Stylwell of Farnham, weaver, was indicted for petty larceny and was charged with breaking into the close of John Lydger at Tilford on 23rd February, killing a sheep and stealing its skin worth 10 pence. He was found not guilty.

A more serious case was brought before the coroner at an 'inquisition' held at Tilford on 24th August 1587 on the body of Margery Shrobbe of Tilford, spinster. The record goes on to say:

> "A jury - William Payne, Thomas May (alias Reves), William Moon, Richard Harding, Richard Hitchcock, Edward Barton, John (?), Thomas Harding, Thomas Preston, Richard Bradbridge, Alexander Lagg, Richard Novell and John West - found that on 23rd August, John Woods of Binsted, Hants, yeoman, entered the house of John Inwood at Tilford, carrying a loaded birding piece (10 shillings). He put the gun down on the table and as he did so it accidentally went off, killing Shrobbe who was standing nearby."

Regrettably, the record is damaged and we do not know the conclusion of this very sad affair.

A further example giving names of Tilford inhabitants is the report of the Commissioners of Sewers (appointed by Elizabeth I) who, around 1565, visited the area to prepare a report on the state of the bridges over the river Wey. The names of those in Tilford who are mentioned in the report's findings on obstructions in the river between Tilford and Elstead include on the south side William Lussher; and on the north side, Edward Stovold, Mary Harding, Harry Boxfold, Steven Hampton, Thomas May, Richard Hitchcock, Robert Chitty, William Luff and Edward Barton (the last-named described in the Commissioners' report as "very evil"!). Seven of these were indicted for 'suffering a tree lying across the river' and Edward Stovold was castigated for this and 'divers other annoyances'. The Commissioners made continued attempts to extract a fine of five shillings from him; the fine was eventually raised to ten shillings but there is no record of whether it was actually paid.

By the Statute of Westminster 1285, confirmed in 1511, all able-bodied men aged between sixteen and sixty were required, according to their means and status, to be equipped with weapons, and skilled in their use. From time to time they were required to muster for inspection and listing and such Muster Lists have been preserved for Farnham Hundred over a number of years of Elizabeth I's reign. Comparing the names on these for Tilford with those on the Rent Rolls and the Lay Subsidies lists gives a useful insight into the make-up of the village. Whilst most properties were being farmed by tenants as occupiers, Chapel Farm, Earls, Hatch, Tilhill, Widemead and Woodhill had been sub-let by the principal tenants.

On the basis of 12 bondland tenants and say 8 other families in the village, we can estimate a population for Tilford in 1594 of around 85. The figure calculated in the previous chapter for the population of Tilford in 1332 was 135 where it was noted that the Black Death had resulted in the deaths of at least 70% of the heads of households. As has been already discussed, conditions of weather, land use, economics and political stability were inimical to population growth over the whole of the fifteenth century, both nationally and locally, and Tilford's population would have remained virtually static during that time.

Overall, the pattern of farming life in Tilford continued without significant change over Tudor times. Land was bought and sold but generally this took place between the village's existing tenants, often as a result of widowhood and remarriage. In many ways the village was a 'closed shop' and it was not until the 17th century, and particularly as a result of the Civil War, that new people came in as tenants of the bondlands. On the other hand, there was much sub-letting - sometimes of parts of the holding and sometimes of the whole area under cultivation. Bridgeland, which had been left as an area of common grazing, was taken in hand and let to William Moon on condition that an annual payment of 3s. 4d. would be made to the burgesses of Farnham for the maintenance of Tilford's bridges. Other areas that had been left without a tenant were also reclaimed.

24. Bridgeland (Malthouse) Farm House, Tilford

The Black Death of 1348 to 1351 left many farms in Tilford derelict. Bridgeland was abandoned and was used as a common grazing ground for villagers in Tilford for many years. In 1575 it was acquired by William Moon on condition that he made an annual payment of 13s 4d. to the Burgesses of Farnham to keep the bridges at Tilford in good repair. Malthouse Farm House was probably built shortly afterwards.

When Elizabeth I died in 1603, Tilford had settled into a peaceful, ordered, existence where everyone knew his or her place and the part he or she had to play in the scheme of things. True, religious practices had changed and Waverley Abbey was now under 'new management', but the established pattern of agricultural life was very much as it had always been. Outside influences stemming from exploration and discovery overseas had not yet percolated through to the rural community of the village and communications, even with Farnham, were tenuous. In the next century, the Civil War would shake up the villagers from their tranquil state and introduce new people with new ideas. Tilford would grow in size and have to prepare to meet the challenges of an emerging industrial world.

Chapter 9

The Civil War and its Aftermath

The start of the 17th century saw Tilford in the hands of a small number of tenants farming the same bondlands that had been worked since 'ancient' times. The devastation wrought by the Black Death, 250 years earlier, was now very much a thing of the past and a flourishing wool trade with its emphasis on sheep farming had brought new life to the village. Purpresture land that had been left uncultivated for want of labour had been brought back into use and standards of living were rising. Unhappily, this was to be short-lived. The three chief towns of West Surrey - Guildford, Godalming and Farnham - had come to depend exclusively on wool, and the livelihood of a great many of their inhabitants depended on the production of kersie, made from the short stapled wool of the Downland sheep. Fashion changes in both London and the export market focused on worsted cloth which required a different kind of wool for its production and the early seventeenth century saw a serious decline in Farnham's wool-textile industry with inevitable consequences for the surrounding villages. Added to this, halfway through the century came the two Civil Wars that imposed heavy burdens on the villagers - both fiscal and through having the forced billeting of Cromwell's soldiers imposed on them. It was not until the third quarter of the century that Tilford was able to recover.

There are a number of records for Tilford over this century that give the names of individuals, and which illuminate relative differences between Tilford and other places in Surrey. From these, together with the Farnham Parish records (which started to include references to the places of domicile of the parishioners towards the end of the 17th century) it is possible to draw conclusions on who owned or occupied the houses in Tilford, their affluence, and the village's prosperity compared with elsewhere. In general, the tenants in Tilford fell into two categories: those like the Novells and the Reves, who farmed the land themselves and lived in the village; and others, such as William Westbrook of Ferring, Sussex, John Coldham and William Aislabie of Waverley Abbey House newly-built on higher ground above the Abbey ruins, and Nicholas Turner of Farnham, who employed others to farm their lands for them. In general, the Civil Wars and their aftermath

(1642 to 1660) had no dramatic effect on landholding, with many family names continuing in possession both before and afterwards.

25. Bridge House (Bridge Farm), Tilford

In 1599, Oliver & Richard Gregory acquired a plot of land by Tilford's East Bridge '6 perches by 2 perches' (100 feet by 33 feet) plus $^1/_2$ acre of land 'to build a house'. The result was a five-bay framed Yeoman's House of 5 hearths. Called Bridge House and very little altered, it has been contiuously occupied since 1601.

There are few direct references to the part played by Tilford in the Civil Wars, but with the Royalist and Parliamentarian campaigns focusing heavily on Farnham and its castle, the village inevitably got drawn in to the conflict. Initially, Farnham castle was taken over by the Deputy-Lieutenants of Surrey in support of the Parliamentary cause but having been abandoned shortly afterwards as its garrison sought to acquire arms in London, it was immediately occupied by Royalist forces under the newly appointed High Sheriff of Surrey. In December 1642 the Roundheads, under Sir William Waller, stormed the castle and secured it for the Parliamentarians, making it a staging point for the assembly of his artillery train. It has been reported that cannons mounted by the Parliamentarians on the top of Crooksbury Hill were responsible, in part, for bringing down Jay's Tower in Farnham Park during the siege of the castle but this seems to be an extravagant claim.

In the light of widespread local Royalist victories in the south east of England, the parliamentary authorities concluded that the Farnham contingent required considerable strengthening and in 1643 Farnham became a garrison town for the Roundheads. Troops were brought in from far afield and thousands of Roundheads converged on the town. In July 1643 a regiment of foot under Colonel Samuel Jones was ordered into Surrey from the Earl of Essex's army with orders to recruit from the county; its headquarters was to be at Farnham. The regiment mustered between 800 and 900 officers and men and was later supported by a number of troops of horse. In October of that year, a new army some 4,000 strong was raised under Sir William Waller with its rendezvous of Farnham.

All these required accommodation and a supply of food. Although references to soldiers being billeted in Tilford are rarely found, records of such billeting in Elstead have been well preserved and it can be safely assumed that Tilford had similar experiences. There is no doubt that the villagers were hard-pressed to meet the demands of the military at this time. Henry Ireton, a general under his father-in-law Oliver Cromwell, is reported to have made his headquarters at Tilhill Farm when the Parliamentary army under Sir William Waller was besieging Farnham Castle, and Cromwell himself is said to have visited the farm, whilst his staff would have found accommodation nearby. The table used by Oliver Cromwell on his visit to Tilhill is said to have been preserved and found its way to Whitmead in the 19th century when it was reported to be in the possession of Colonel Davis.

The billeting of soldiers in and around Farnham had been a source of friction well before the start of the Civil Wars and there is no doubt that it was a major source of discontent during the wars. On January 28th 1628, Charles I's office issued the following rebuke: "One hundred and thirty soldiers were sent out of Hants to be billeted at Farnham, without order from the Council. Pray that, in consideration of their expense in billeting soldiers, and also in conveying 1,000 soldiers which have lately passed through Surrey, these soldiers may be removed from Farnham, which town is greatly impoverished through the plague and many charges." On July 7th 1628, Charles I's office refers to the billeting of soldiers in Farnham and remonstrates: "When at Farnham, the Bishop gave the town his word for repayment of their billets. Since then the inhabitants have been so refractory that they have turned some of the soldiers out of doors and persuaded others to do the like. Pray for a Council Warrant to billet the soldiers in the town."

In November the Royalist Army comprising some 8,000 men attacked the castle defended by Waller but were repulsed, and with winter bringing a halt to further campaigning Waller's army sat out the winter in West Sussex. On 17th April 1644, Waller and his army returned to Farnham and once again, the town and the surrounding villages had to bear the burden of supporting them. In May the army departed, returning in August at half strength after a series of defeats. The winter of 1644/45 and 1645/46 saw further heavy demands made on Farnham and the villages. In particular, the harvest of 1645 was poor and the dispossessed and homeless soldiers experienced starvation and exposure. Associations of local people banded together to protect property and goods from marauding soldiers many of whom quartered themselves indiscriminately in the area. Some of them, particularly those from the London regiments, were unruly at best and as the war dragged on, became an increasing source of friction and disturbance. A letter written by William Cawley (a Chichester brewer and Member of Parliament) from Farnham on November 23rd 1643 refers to Waller's soldiers in the following terms: "their abounding vices and enormities.... produce.... great discontent.... to the country, from which they are sometimes necessitated to take that for their livelihood which the people can ill spare".

Records from Elstead show that much difficulty was experienced by the villagers in supplying provisions and fodder for horses. On the other hand, taxes were paid regularly under order of Act of Parliament. There is nothing to indicate that any monies were raised to support the Royalist cause and it has been suggested that this indicates that the villagers were Parliamentary supporters, but it perhaps more likely reflected the feelings of the local landowners influenced, as they were, by Parliamentary troops occupying Farnham and the surrounding villages.

At the cessation of hostilities in August 1646, there was widespread relief in the belief that the normal pattern of farming life could resume. It must have been with much dismay that trouble broke out again the following year and there were reports of Royalist uprisings. Fortunately for Tilford, these did not materialise locally and although Farnham itself was intimately involved in the plight of Charles I who fled through the town after escaping from Hampton Court Palace (and who was eventually brought back from his sanctuary in the Isle of Wight, stopping overnight in Farnham), the village was not involved and suffered none of the hardships of the first war.

The Interregnum under Cromwell had little impact on Tilford but the village took a long time to recover from its wartime ordeals. Although Farnham's role as a garrison town had stimulated industry, the decline in the wool-textile industry, which had collapsed in the 1620's, led to an economic depression in the area by 1640. Added to this, some bad harvests and a particularly severe fresh outbreak of the plague had brought the countryside to a new low. All this hit Tilford hard and it was not until Charles the Second was restored to the throne in 1660 that the prosperity of the village started to recover.

The source of this recovery was a revival of the corn trade. The decline in cloth manufacture had left many fulling mills idle and in a reversal of what had occurred previously, they found a new role in grinding corn. Farnham found itself the centre of a new and growing corn market. So much so that Daniel Defoe in his travels through Britain in the early part of the next century was compelled to say the Farnham was "without exception the greatest corn-market in England, London excepted", a sentiment echoed by John Aubrey in his survey of Surrey begun in 1673.

In 1662, Charles II introduced a hearth tax under which "all houses in this Kingdom which are not worth in yearly value below twenty shillings and not inhabited by Almsmen must pay your Majesty two shillings yearly for every chimney hearth for ever." The 'for ever' was a trifle over-ambitious since the tax was abolished twenty-seven years later, but over that time a number of assessments for the tax were made and have been preserved. In particular, those for 1669/70 and 1673/4 are complete for Tilford and give the names of the residents. These records enable a good assessment to be made of numbers in the village but also of the wealth of the villagers and how well they were faring compared with their neighbours.

Tilford boasted one house of 5 hearths, one of 4, ten of 3, two of 2, and four of 1 - of which three were ascribed to non-chargeable 'paupers'. It is possible to allocate present-day names to many of these listings. A comparison with other tithings of Farnham Hundred shows that Tilford was one of the better-off villages with only one-sixth of its numbers below the poverty line. Surprisingly, the worst village was Frensham where one-half were officially designated 'paupers'; for the Hundred as a whole the figure was 40%.

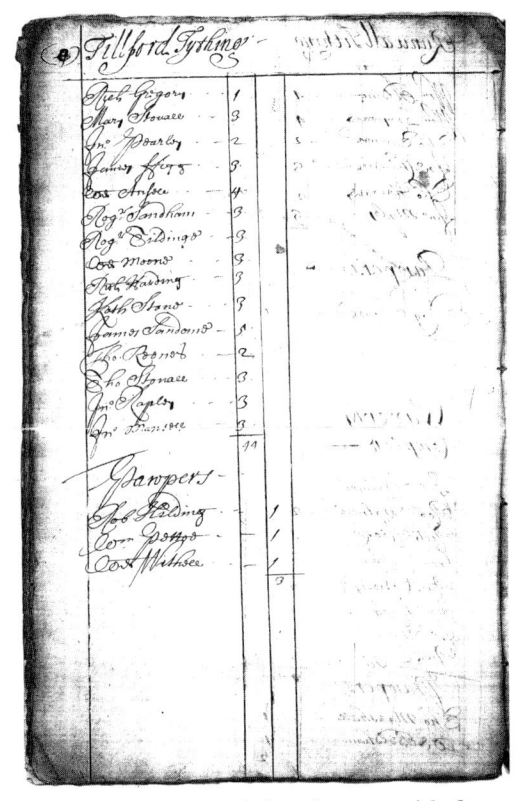

26. Hearth Tax Record for Tilford Tithing A.D. 1669/70

(reproduced by permission of the Public Record Office E 179/258/4 22272)

The Hearth Tax record listed the number of hearths in each house and gave the names of the tenants, who were divided into payees and 'paupers', who were exempt payment. The tax was two shillings per hearth per year. Tilford in 1669 had one house (Bridge House) with 5 hearths, ten with 3 hearths, two with 2 hearths and four with 1 hearth. (It is thought that the house with 4 hearths (Widow Ansell) was included in Tilford's list in error).

It has been suggested that houses with fewer than three hearths were below the comfortable level, those with more than ten were in a state of considerable affluence. Tilford, with its range from 1 to 5 and majority having 3, is clearly at the just-comfortable level expected for the none-too-wealthy yeoman farmer of the day. In Farnham town, leaving aside the Bishop's residence at the castle and lodge, there were nine houses with 5 hearths, six with 6, seven with 7, six with 8 and two with 9. Elsewhere, except for the grand houses in Frensham, Moor Park and Waverley Abbey, there were rarely any houses with more than 5 hearths. Thus, outside the town of Farnham itself, there were no 'privileged' areas other than these three wealthy country properties.

A comparison of the Lay Subsidies tax paid by the villages between 1594 and 1677 reveals which parts of the area grew in prosperity over that time and which declined. Farnham town itself contributed only 28% of the total for the Hundred in 1677 compared with 35% in 1594; similarly Tilford fell from $3^1/_2$% to $2^1/_2$%. Churt, Elstead and Frensham did particularly well in spite of their large 'pauper' populations - leading to the conclusion that either these were even greater in 1594 than in 1677 or that the wealth of these places was unevenly distributed. It is of interest to note that in those Lay Subsidies where the occupations of taxpayers are given, no craftsmen or tradesmen are ever listed for Tilford. Thus, we are left with a picture of Tilford, with its relatively small number of paupers and apparent absence of craft workers, as a tightly bound, evenly matched, community relying exclusively on farming. Whilst farming continued to be Tilford's sole activity, the next century saw Tilford's wealth becoming concentrated into fewer hands as land holdings began to be amalgamated into large estates, with the number of landlords reducing by the end of that century to a mere handful.

Chapter 10

The Landed Gentry

The eighteenth century was a time of increasing prosperity for Tilford. The success of Farnham's corn market in the 17th century had spread out beyond the town and successful merchants expanded their interests by buying land in the villages. However, as the eighteenth century advanced, Farnham saw a serious decline in this market. Guildford had also converted from wool to corn and being in a more central location than Farnham, and with a navigable waterway to London, rose in importance to the detriment of Farnham's trade. The townsfolk clearly saw their salvation lay in promoting the cultivation of hops, which had remained latent since its introduction in the 16th century. In 1700, corn dominated the market but by 1800 hops had taken over and the corn trade in Farnham had severely declined. Farnham achieved wide recognition for the quality of its hops and was able to command much higher prices at market than elsewhere in the country. This reputation was jealously guarded and the Farnham 'trademark' was restricted to within the borders of the town. Outlying villages, such as Tilford, tried to follow suit but were not able to capitalise fully on the popularity of Farnham hops and did not turn exclusively to this crop like the growers in Farnham for whom hop-growing was their sole or principal object. Nevertheless, hop growing did slowly spread out to the villages and by latching on to the coat tails of Farnham, Tilford undoubtedly prospered from its success and growing wealth.

In the latter half of the eighteenth century a number of reports on the state of Surrey's farming emerged and from these it is possible to gain some impression of how Tilford would have looked at this time. Away from the village would have been near limitless heathland and descriptions abound on its nature and appearance. William Marshall, writing in 1798, describes the area as 'barren lands'. He goes on to say:

> "The soil of the whole of these heathy wastes...is a barren sand or gravel; encrusted with the black earth of heaths, of a dry crumbly quality; and in general, very thin; the soil altogether being of the

very worst quality...The flat, between Farnham and Godalming is, almost literally, a barren waste, a sandy desert."

Within this 'desert', the river's alluvial deposits combined with man's energies over many centuries had set oases of more fertile land such as Tilford and a range of crops were grown. Although records are not separately available for the village, figures for the whole of Farnham Parish (but excluding hops - the major income-producing crop) were reported at the end of the century. They show that the areas devoted to wheat, barley and oats were broadly equal, whilst rye was hardly grown at all. Of the legumes and root crops, peas took by far the largest area, followed by turnips, beans, and potatoes.

Marshall describes the livestock of the local area as 'inconsiderable'; cattle, he says, are 'small mean-looking' but 'of a quality intrinsically good' and in the neighbourhood of Farnham are 'the longhorned breed'. Surprisingly, in view of the earlier dominance of sheep, Marshall describes numbers of these also as 'inconsiderable'. Once again, he uses the term 'mean' and describes them as "small, mean, ill formed animals" but goes on to say that "their mutton, however, is in high repute. And they are probably well fleshed; having been *starved* into their present state". The only thing that Marshall commends is fish in the various fishponds (such as Abbot's Pond) and he suggests that "large tracts of this worthless land [might] be profitably covered with deep water.... as a source of fish"! Of wild life, Marshall comments merely on the absence of rabbits; and this is surprising considering that the area south of Tilford was once the site of the Bishop of Winchester's warren. The main pest of the time was the hedgehog. Year after year, the Farnham Parish accounts record money paid out for the carcasses of these animals together with those of 'sparrows and other small birds' which, presumably, were ruining the seed planting. In a more prophetic mood, Marshall suggested that the land might have much more potential if coniferous trees (he proposed the larch) were to be planted and nurtured on the 'unculturable land'. This was started on Crooksbury Hill in 1776 and its development since has had the result of making Surrey the most wooded county in the land.

All this speaks of poor returns from the land but this is without taking into account hops. Although Farnham hops were highly prized and frequently fetched one-third above, and sometimes double, the price in other areas, those grown in Tilford, being outside the select Farnham boundary, would not have been as valuable. However, the increased prosperity of Farnham town arising from its hop trade had its effects on the surrounding area and Tilford, along with other outlying parts of the parish, profited from its neighbour's influence and wealth.

27. Tilford House 1854
(reproduced by permission of Surrey History Service SHC 1576/74/1)

This Picture is taken from a watercolour of Tilford House painted by Martin Ware in 1854. The house today has been enlarged by two matching wings, the one on the west being added around 1900 and the other on the east in 1992.

A prime example of how Tilford benefited from such wealth came in 1727 when John Turner a mercer in Petworth, Sussex, the grandson of Nicholas Turner a mealman from Farnham who had made his money from the corn trade, built Tilford House - the first 'grand house' to be built in the village. Nicholas had earlier acquired sizeable areas of land in Tilford from his uncle William Perry, and his son Stephen, a pewterer, having predeceased him, had passed them on directly to his grandson. John Turner lived in the house for the four years left to him and when he died in 1731 the house and lands passed to his mother Mary and his three sisters Rebecca, Mary and Dorothy. They jointly decided they would sell the property and in 1732 it was bought for under £2,700 by Peter Green of Walthamstow in Essex, described simply as 'gentleman'. Peter stayed in the House (acquiring further property in Tilford during his time there) until 1752 when he moved out to Ratcliffe Cross in Middlesex.

In 1761, Tilford House and its lands was bought by Elizabeth Abney and a process of relentless acquisition in Tilford was started that eventually was to end up with over a third of the village being part of the Tilford House estate. Elizabeth Abney was a spinster, the daughter of Sir Thomas Abney, by his second wife Mary Gunston. Sir Thomas made a name for himself in the City of London, being knighted by William III and rising to be Lord Mayor in 1770, the first non-conformist to be elected to this position. His first marriage produced seven children of whom six died in infancy or early youth and the seventh at the age of 24. From his marriage to Mary Gunston, Sir Thomas had three daughters, and after his death in 1722, Elizabeth, born in 1704 and being the last to survive, became the sole heiress to the considerable fortunes of both her parents. Her main residence was Abney House in the manor of Stoke Newington in London and she acquired Tilford House in 1761as a summer residence. Her reason for coming to Tilford is not at all clear. She had inherited her father's non-conformist beliefs and was an ardent dissenter; Nicholas Turner was also a dissenter, and it may be that he and Sir Thomas set up some acquaintanceship, which led to Elizabeth being aware of the property at Tilford. Whatever the case, Elizabeth bought the house and its contents - which Peter Green had furnished in style - at auction in London for £4,188.4s.6d (the £188 odd was for the contents), and took an active interest in the village, enlarging and extending her estate

When Elizabeth came to Tilford each summer, she brought with her her Chaplain, the Reverend Thomas Tayler, a non-conformist minister. As a fervent believer she wished to practise her religion at home and very early on petitioned the Bishop of Winchester for a licence to enable the Reverend Tayler to conduct Divine Service in Tilford House. The 'Great House', as it was then described, was a square building without the two wings that were to be added later on. The entrance at the front led into an imposing hall and it was here that the Reverend Tayler conducted his services. Keen to be able to offer such services to a larger congregation, Elizabeth Abney approached the bishop for permission to erect a separate building for divine worship in the grounds of Tilford House. This was granted in 1776 and the small chapel, which still stands in the grounds, was built in the same year - the first purpose-built place of worship to be erected in the village.

28. Portrait of Reverend Thomas Tayler (1735 - 1831) Chaplain to Elizabeth Abney (reproduced by permission of Surrey History Service SHC 1576/34/1)

A wealthy man living in Bedford Row and owning an estate in Worcestershire and a house and farm in Ash, Thomas Tayler inherited the Tilford House estate from Elizabeth Abney in 1783.

Whilst pressing for the chapel to be built, Elizabeth Abney commissioned a survey to be made of her Tilford estate. The surveyors she chose were George Cobbett, the father of his more famous son William, and John Jarrett. The survey was completed in 1767 and the drawing, which accompanied the survey, is the first large-scale accurate map of Tilford ever made. Included in the 1761 sale of the Tilford House Estate, were Wanford, Tuney, Tilford House Farm, Rede, part of Tilford virgate, and land north of the river further along from Whitmead towards Elstead - covering, in all, some 185 acres. In 1770, Elizabeth Abney also acquired Tilford Green Cottages, the original of which (No 1), a quarter of a century previously, had been extended eastwards to form a second cottage (No 2). An even earlier (c1715) extension westwards, which had become Tilford's first inn, the Barley Mow, was not part of the deal. Later on, in 1775, she purchased from Thomas Matchwick the 79-acre Chapel Farm, which she added to her estate. George Cobbett and John Jarrett were again called upon to prepare a survey and a second map was produced in 1776 showing the extent of Chapel Farm, where a new walk besides the coppices had been constructed. The map included Stockbridge Pond, which she had also acquired. Two years later, in August 1782, the grand old lady died, aged 78, leaving the bulk of her estate in London to be sold and the proceeds to be distributed amongst poor individuals or corporate charities. The Tilford properties she left to her faithful Chaplain, Thomas Tayler.

29. Tilford House Chapel

Built by Elizabeth Abney in the grounds of Tilford House in 1776, Tilford House Chapel was Tilford's first purpose-built place of worship. It has continued in use but lapsed as a place for public religious services after the Bishop of Winchester withdrew his licence for the performance of divine service in 1842.

The Reverend Tayler resided in the 'Great House' for some 5 years but in 1789, perhaps because of rising costs, decided to move elsewhere and he offered the house up for rent. His tenants up to the end of the century were first Captain Thomas Everett, succeeded by the Marquis of Lothian, Mrs Hamilton, and Mrs Munro. The land meanwhile was being farmed by the same sub-tenants as had worked under Miss Abney. Thomas Tayler introduced no changes in the estate, either by sale or purchase, and unlike Elizabeth Abney, appears to have taken little direct interest in the village. A daughter, Anne, was born to the Reverend and Mrs Tayler on June 11th 1792 and it is to her, in the next century, that we have to look for the development of the Tilford House estate and the influence its owner was to have on Tilford and its inhabitants.

Outside of the Tilford House estate, other properties were also being drawn together. Four families competed for dominance - the Moons, the Mansells, the Matchwicks and the Stovolds. Of these, the first three, who together early on owned Bridgeland, Chapel Farm, Coopers, Fishers, Hidemead, Squires Hill Farm, Threshers, Tilford, and Woodhill, were all interconnected through marriage. Standing outside of them, was the Stovold family that was to be, in the end, the principal competitor alongside Tilford House in the ownership of land in Tilford.

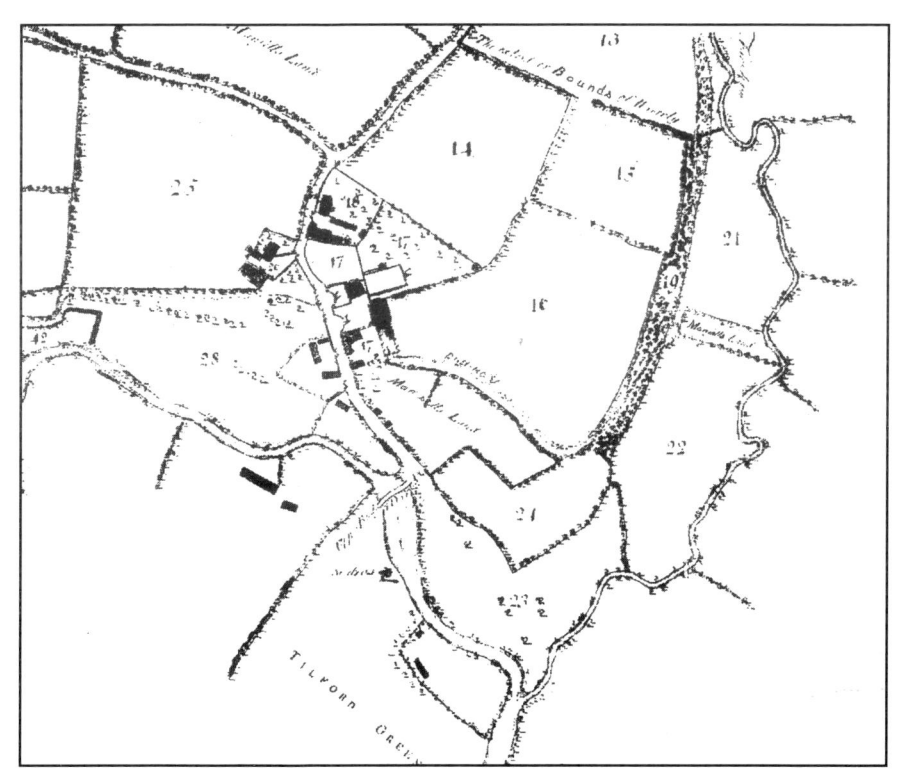

30. Part of the map of Elizabeth Abney's Estate in Tilford prepared by George Cobbett and John Jarrett in 1767.
(reproduced by permission of Surrey History Service SHC 1487/23/4)

In 1762 John Rocque produced a map of Surrey at a scale of 2 inches to the mile. Although this was the first map to show Tilford in some detail, it is not wholly accurate and Cobbett and Jarrett's drawing is recognised as the first reliable large-scale map depicting the western part of Tilford.

The name of Stovold first appears locally in 1269; by the 17th century, members of the family were present in many villages around Farnham - in particular Elstead, Compton and Tilford. The Stovold name first appears in the Tilford records in Edward VI's reign when Edward Stovold married the widow of William Westbrook, thus acquiring Woodhill and Earls. Around 1580, having given up Woodhill and Earls to his stepson, he took over Tilhill leaving that, in turn, to his son Henry when he died. Henry, himself, died in 1609 and his widow, Mary, took over the Tilford properties. By 1730, there were three branches of the family in Tilford in possession of Earls, Linches, Tilhill, Widebrooks and Widemead. By the end of the 18th

31. Anne Tayler
(1792 - 1859)

(reproduced by permission of Surrey History Service SHC 1487/115/3)

The daughter of the Reverend Thomas Tayler, Chaplain to Elizabeth Abney, Anne married Martin Ware in 1816 and was the mother of James Ware and grandmother of Martin Stewart Ware, successive owners of Tilford House.

century, the Stovold's Tilford estate stretched across much of the land east of the river and the two protagonists for land, the Stovolds and the owners of Tilford House, had become well matched.

Alone in all this was Sheephatch, which was acquired by the owner of Waverley Abbey, Thomas Orby Hunter, in 1751 and was to remain as part of the Waverley Abbey estate until 1947. Thomas Hunter was the first of the Waverley owners to expand the estate by moving into Tilford, reversing the policy of his predecessor John Coldham who had sold Wanford to Robert Palmer a hundred years previously. In 1754, he bought an additional 10 acres of land on the top and south-west side of Crooksbury hill where he started to plant trees. It was his successor Lieutenant-General Sir Robert Rich, however, who had distinguished himself at the battle of Culloden Moor, who extended and developed this practice. In 1774, he took up 15 more acres of waste on Crooksbury hill from the summit down to the road and two years later planted it with four-year old Scotch Firs set 4 feet apart. This was a radical new venture and one that was to be copied widely in the area over the ensuing years. It was certainly very profitable. Sir Robert paid the Bishop the princely sum of £5 for his 15 acres (Thomas Hunter had only paid 5 shillings for his earlier 10 acres). Twelve years later it was valued at £8 an acre and at the turn of the century the number of trees was estimated to stand at 16,624 and were valued at £1,281.10s.0d. In 1778, he went further and acquired 30 acres of waste on the other side of Waverley between Redhill and Tilford. All this was to radically change the appearance of the countryside to the north of Tilford from extensive heathland to the pinewoods we see today.

Whilst Sir Robert's development plans were wreaking great changes to the environment, they were not always popular. William Cobbett who worked as a garden boy at Waverley when Sir Robert arrived, was particularly scathing about his actions in the Abbey grounds. Writing in his book 'The English Gardener' he says that whilst Rich's predecessors "had had the good taste to leave the ancient gardens, the grange, and as much of the old walls of the convent as was, standing" and that it was then "one of the most beautiful and interesting spots in the world", when Sir Robert arrived he:
"tore everything to atoms, except the remaining wall of the convent itself. He even removed the high hill at the back of the valley; actually carried it away in carts and wheel barrows; built a new-fashioned mansion-house with grey bricks, made the place as bare as possible; and in defiance of nature and all the hoar of antiquity, made it little better than a vulgar box of a cockney."

The Farnham Churchwarden's also had their criticism of Sir Robert. In the Parish accounts for September 1780 it is recorded that the Vestry met 'to consider Sir Robert Rich's proposals regarding the turning of a road near Waverley Mill.' The Vestry directed the Surveyor of the Highways to immediately give notice "to the said Robert Rich to open the foot road leading from Compton Waverley to Tilford and the replace the bridge that he has illegally pulled down".

The power of Farnham Vestry had increased considerably since the beginning of the eighteenth century. This was partly because of a lack of enterprise shown by the bailiffs and burgesses of Farnham Corporation - the other source of administrative power in the parish - but perhaps more directly because of the decline in their income which depended on the toll on corn which had seriously fallen since the early part of the century. The Corporation was a closed one, supposed to fill its own numbers. This they neglected to do, and the two bailiffs and twelve burgesses dwindled to six or seven in the latter part of the century. At last, in 1789, Mr William Shotter, an attorney, was the sole remaining member. Outgoings had exceeded income on occasions and he had ended up paying out of his own pocket. Finally, because of expenses connected with Tilford, he decided to 'dissolve himself' and surrendered the charters and all the documents of the corporation into the hands of the then Bishop of Winchester, Brownlow North.

The expenses at Tilford which precipitated the winding up of Farnham Corporation were the repairs to Tilford's bridges which, by an arrangement instituted in 1574, were subsidised by the tenant of Bridgeland who was required to pay 13 shillings and 4 pence each year to the Farnham bailiffs for their upkeep. At its inception, the sum of 13s. 4d. was a reasonable sum to pay; as the centuries advanced it became derisory - but it was religiously paid nevertheless right up to the end.

In addition to maintenance of the bridges, under an Act of Elizabeth I, parishes were responsible for the upkeep of roads that ran through them. The tracks providing the excuse for roads in Surrey were notoriously bad and most goods to and from Tilford had to be carried by packhorses. South of Tilford lay the barren heathlands and the tracks to Farnham and Elstead were the only sensible routes open for travellers in and out of the village. From 1751, when the navigable section of the Wey was extended to Godalming, goods such as timber were taken there from Farnham via Elstead. Later, in 1794, the Basingstoke Canal was completed and 'Farnham Wharf' north of Aldershot became the loading point for goods going by barge to and from London. In the country at large, roads had not seen any deliberate skilled engineering or construction since Roman times. The first major advance was the introduction of toll roads, or turnpikes, which were brought in in the 17th century. The first turnpike road to reach Farnham was constructed in 1758 by improving the existing road to Guildford where it connected with other turnpikes that went through Leatherhead to London. This had a dramatic effect on transport and wheeled vehicles steadily replaced packhorses to and from the capital, with mail coaches being introduced in 1784. A journey which in 1700 took 6 days was reduced, by 1750, to 3 days; seventy years later this came down to 28 hours. Tilford steadily became less isolated as travel to the Capital improved.

Whilst the passage of legitimate goods improved, so did that of contraband. The duties charged on foreign imports such as tobacco, wine, proof spirits, teas and sugar in the 18th century made smuggling a profitable if dangerous enterprise. So secret a trade has left little firm evidence and what is available about the local area all stems from memories about the eighteenth century that have been recorded in the nineteenth. There is general agreement that contraband goods smuggled through Tilford came from the

Sussex coast and were being transported to Bagshot Heath. What happened at Bagshot is not revealed. Presumably the contraband was off-loaded to dealers who had profitable markets to satisfy in London. As can be appreciated, the route taken was clandestine and followed none of the established tracks. To keep such activity hidden, it was necessary to bribe the locals along the route and there is good evidence to suppose that defrauding the Customs and Excise was considered to be no great crime and many god-fearing folk joined in the process. Many country houses got their supplies of spirits and wines from smugglers and it was considered no great disgrace to do so.

The route taken by the smugglers can be gleaned from the scraps of evidence available. The Surrey landscape in the 18th century was marked by vast expanses of barren heath and it would not have been difficult for smugglers to have travelled through this undetected, particularly at night. After the imported contraband goods arrived off the Sussex coast and were unloaded, they went from there by diverse routes to the Surrey border close to Haslemere. The smugglers then had to cross the London-to-Portsmouth Road at a hidden spot before moving north over Hindhead and Frensham Commons. Crossing the Wey at Frensham was the next hurdle. The bridge at Millbridge was too exposed and so the smugglers with their heavily laden packhorses and ponies opted for Tancred's Ford. From there they had to reach Seale and analysis suggests that the route ran across Tancredsford Common to reach Sheephatch Lane where the smugglers were able to ford the other branch of the Wey. From there they went towards Crooksbury, up 'Smugglers' Way' to Seale via the Sands. From Seale they travelled north crossing the Hog's Back with care and circumspection until, once past Ash, they had uninterrupted heath land all the way to Bagshot.

One of the properties on the route of the smugglers was Pierrepont Lodge, built in the 1750's overlooking Tancred's ford, and acquired by Ralph Wood in 1785. Wood, a man of considerable wealth, pulled down the house and built himself a fine new one half a mile closer to Millbridge which he called Highfield (the present day Pierrepont Christian Training Centre). It is recorded that he did this to place himself at a safe distance from the smuggling fraternity who could well have brought him embarrassment, if not danger and scandal. Ralph Wood lost his money through the misdeeds of his son-in-law, John Tayler, an East India merchant in whom Wood had invested his fortune. It is said that, in addition to his other questionable activities, Tayler was a great smuggler. Wood's other daughter married Crawford Davison who resided in Tilford House from 1813 to 1821 - but there is no question of his ever being involved in smuggling.

Whilst Tilford advanced in material ways, its social and religious side was not neglected. The villager's parish church was St Andrew's in Farnham - although St James's in Elstead was closer, particularly for those at Charles Hill. Attending church, four miles away, was a major undertaking and the arrival of Elizabeth Abney and her chaplain, Thomas Tayler, in Tilford in 1761 and the construction, five years later, of a dedicated chapel in the grounds of Tilford House brought many to worship there rather than travel, mostly on foot, to Farnham. At the Bishop's Visitation of St Andrew's in 1725, the newly-arrived Vicar of Farnham, James Forde, reported that, in a parish population of 2,500, Protestant dissenters in the parish numbered 80 with a further 30 Anabaptists and 12 Quakers. At the next visitation in 1788, James Jackson, the then Farnham Vicar, reported that there were 'very few' dissenters in a population that had risen to 3000. This was perhaps wishful thinking and did not take into account the situation in places such as Tilford, which were some distance away from the town.

This is not to say that Tilford was isolated from Farnham. Rates and taxes were still rigorously collected, as is clearly identified in the accounts of the Farnham Church Wardens. In the early part of the century, the rate was generally set at 3 pence in the pound on the assessed value of property. Twenty-five properties in Tilford contributed and the sum realised from the village in 1728 was £2.10s.0d. For Farnham Parish as a whole, the town contributed £29.8s.1^{1}/$_{2}$d and the country £24.9s.6^{3}/$_{4}$d, making a total annual income to the Vestry of £53.17s.7^{1}/$_{4}$d. The ratio of the amount levied on Tilford to that on Farnham Town (*viz* 8^{1}/$_{2}$%) was very little different from what it had been fifty years previously and illustrates the way the wealth of the inhabitants of Tilford had kept pace with that of those from Farnham.

In 1723 a law was enacted which required each parish to erect its own workhouse. Three years later a structure for this purpose was built in Farnham in Middle Church Lane near the east end of St Andrew's churchyard. The following year Nathanial Oldfield was appointed 'Master of the Workhouse and Governor of the Poor' at a salary of £45 per year to include the wages of 'a cook woman'. Alas, he was a most unsuitable choice for, in 1728, we have the following entry in the records: "It appears on examination of two witnesses that Nathanial Oldfield is guilty of several immoralities and the said Vestry hath agreed to discharge him from being Master of the Workhouse within a fortnight next and to pay him a month's wages." Although towards the end of the century an increasing number of Tilford ratepayers were registered as 'poor' and were relieved from payment of rates, there is no record of any of them being sent to the workhouse.

In 1750, the Vestry decided that 'there are certain boys and girls now in the workhouse fit to be placed out as apprentices' and called for 'an account of the indentures of all parish children belonging to the parish of Farnham placed out since 1700'. Out of a total of 122 names of such children, four had been sent to Tilford. John Baker had been apprenticed to John Fox (Earls & Widemead) in 1701, John Beldham to William Moon (Bridgeland) in 1725, John Floyd to George Stovold (Earls) in 1736, and Anne Shrubb to Thomas Stovold (Tilhill) also in 1736. In 1742, Elizabeth Barnett had been appointed to be apprenticed to Henry Mansell (Coopers) but he had refused her. Dennis Cooke was sent out by the Vestry to 'distrain the Mansells goods, he refusing to take a parish boy [sic]'. For this he claimed 2s.6d expenses 'for going to Tilford three times'. One wonders whether this 'distrainment' was worth it.

An increasing problem throughout the parish was that of vagrancy. In 1750, the Farnham Vestry minutes show that:

> "This parish has been for many years past (but very much of late) inflicted with sturdy beggars, rogues, and vagabonds, greatly disturbing the inhabitants.....It is, therefore, adjudged t'will be necessary to make Henry Collins a beadle and allow him with some reasonable salary, to apprehend all such beggars, vagrants, and imposters, and to have them before His Majesty's justices of the Peace, to be punished or otherwise dealt with according to law. It is therefore agreed by us to allow the said Henry Collins a salary of thirty-five shillings, to buy him a coat and hat for that purpose for one year".

Reporting in 1805 on conditions in Surrey, James Malcolm noted that:

> "The labouring poor, as well as the impotent, the aged, and infirm, have been in a progressive state of increase, to a very alarming degree, for several years in this county, but within the last four or five years it has exceeded all credibility......Who can live in the country, or go to the country, without daily seeing gangs if I may so call them of children from the age of six to sixteen sent out to beg and plunder?"

It is not clear to what part of Surrey James Malcolm is referring. It is doubtful that Tilford suffered much in this way although reports from the 19th century show that such unruly behaviour was not far away from the village. Overall, however, the problem of the poor and unemployed was steadily worsening and by 1803, sixteen percent of the inhabitants of Surrey were in receipt of poor relief with the county spending 13s.3d. per head on poor rates. In Tilford the role of Elizabeth Abney and her successors became crucial in ameliorating the plight of the 'labouring poor' in the village and their philanthropy and care for the welfare of the villagers, later augmented by the Andersons at Waverley House, greatly helped to preserve the harmony of the community in the coming century.

Chapter 11

Paternalism and Change

As we move into the 19th century, we find Tilford is still an isolated farming community that has hardly altered in shape or character over the preceding centuries. All this was to change with the arrival of the railway which reached Farnham in 1849. The railway not only brought London much closer and made regular commuting to and from the capital a viable proposition, it also triggered the expansion of Aldershot as a home for the British Army thereby bringing in trade and commerce to the local area on a much larger scale. This, accompanied by a marked improvement in the roads, opened up Tilford to the outside world, and following the enclosure of the commons in 1853, brought developers to the village who saw and benefited from the influx of the 'gentry' from London. Over the century, Tilford changed almost out of all recognition.

The latter part of the 18th century had seen much of Tilford divided up between five landlords: the Reverend Thomas Tayler, who had inherited the Tilford House Estate; John Thomson, the owner of the Waverley Abbey Estate from 1796 to 1830, who had taken over Sheephatch; the Stovolds who owned Earls, Tilhill and Widemead; the Moons who owned Bridgeland, Grovers and Woodhill; and the Mansells who owned most of the rest. Only a few others held land in Tilford - mainly centred around Charles Hill and upon Crooksbury Common - although there were also a few squatters on the moors round about. In 1799, most of the Mansell land was acquired by William Timson, a London merchant who in 1796 had moved into Moor Park. At his departure in 1820, Crawford Davison, who up to then had been living in Tilford House, acquired much of Timson's holdings in Tilford, at the same time buying Highfield Place in Frensham which he renamed Pierrepont. Thomas Tayler died in 1831 and the stage was set for the amalgamation of land that was to become a dominant feature in Tilford during Victoria's reign.

In his will, the Reverend Thomas Tayler left his Tilford properties to his daughter Anne who, in 1816 at the age of 24, had married surgeon oculist Dr Martin Ware. The Ware family, who retained their connections with

Tilford until very recent times, became the dominant influence in Tilford, expanding the Tilford House Estate from the 260 acres inherited by Anne to over 800 acres. The strong religious element that had passed on from Elizabeth Abney through her chaplain, Thomas Tayler, to the Wares reflected the mood of the times and greatly assisted moves to endow Tilford as a separate ecclesiastical parish. Tilford House, with its close affinity with the church authorities and its extensive estate, became the most powerful influence in the village and the Wares played the leading role in all Tilford's affairs.

32. Tilford House c. 1905
(reproduced by permission of Surrey History Service SHC 1487/116/2)

At this time, the west wing had been added to Tilford House and a line of magnificent elm trees lay in front of the house.

The Church pervaded all aspects of village life. With the Bishop of Winchester as Lord of the Manor, owning all of the copyhold land, the Vicar of Farnham, as Archdeacon of Surrey, profiting from all of the tithes, and the Vestry in Farnham exercising its authority over most, if not all, of the parish's activities and functions, the Church was all powerful. Allied to it were the owners of the local 'great houses', Waverley Abbey, Pierrepont, Moor Park and Tilford House; and almost everything relied on patronage. Fortunately for Tilford, the Wares were both fair and benevolent and were genuinely concerned for the welfare of the villagers. There are numerous examples of individual works of charity undertaken by the family and it is to the Wares that the village owes the founding of both church and school.

It was, however, the Dissenting Church that made the first move in providing the village with a public place of worship. In the winter of 1821, the Surrey Mission Society supported by Congregational Dissenters extended their ministry to Tilford and with the help of the villagers, who gave their labour and use of their horses free, built a chapel alongside the village green on land donated by Thomas Tayler who also provided £100 towards the total cost of the building of £420. When the chapel and land was formally handed over to a Board of Trustees in 1823, Martin Ware agreed to be one of the trustees - indicating his strong personal interest in the village a decade before he and his wife inherited Tilford House. The chapel was serviced by Ministers from Elstead and was supported by the Surrey Mission Society until towards the end of the century.

33. Chapel Farmhouse and the Chapel by the Green at Tilford
(reproduced from the Ware family album 31.46 by kind permission of the Old Kiln Museum Trust, Tilford.)

Chapel Farm took its name from the Dissenters' Chapel - shown to the right of the picture - which was erected in 1821. At that time there was an old farmhouse some way to the north closer to the East Bridge. The building on the left of the picture is the new farmhouse, the foundations of which were laid in September 1836 by Dr. Burden, brother-in-law to Anne Ware's sister. Over the years, the congregation at the chapel dwindled and in 1894 the chapel was demolished. The stones from the Chapel were used in the foundations of the Institue that was being built at the same time on the other side of the Green.

In 1827, Bishop Sumner was appointed to Winchester and found the Established Church in Farnham in a most unsatisfactory state. The vicar was non-resident and all the care of this large parish rested on one curate. Bishop Sumner aimed to remedy this situation by the addition of two or three clergymen for work in the parish. Shortly afterwards, he sought permission from Thomas Tayler for the Church of England minister in Seale, the Reverend Frederick Stevens, to conduct services in the chapel that Elizabeth Abney had had built in the grounds of Tilford House.

Despite Tayler being a Presbyterian minister, this was readily agreed, and C of E services were held on Sunday mornings and afternoons alternately to fit in with the services at the dissenting chapel on the green - so that when the C of E service at the house chapel was in the morning, the dissenting service at the chapel on the green was in the afternoon, and vice-versa. The congregations for both were very much the same except that the Nicholsons, who had acquired Waverley Abbey in 1830 and who were Unitarians, attended only the Church of England services. Mr Emmett, of Chapel Farm, officiated at both chapels. Mr Charles Ware, son of Martin and Anne Ware recounts: "The men sat on the left hand of the house chapel in their smock frocks with the women on the other side. There were three pews, one for the house, one for the Nicholsons, and one for Mr Harris and his family [the principal farmer of the Tilford House Estate]. The Stovolds, a family of yeomen cultivating their own land, sat in a corner near the pulpit."

In 1832, the cottage opposite Tilford House (Tilford Cottage) became vacant, and the Reverend Stevens occupied it with the result that Tilford had, for the first time, a resident Church of England minister. A succession of such ministers was to follow: R W Johnson in 1837, Henry Dodds in 1838 and Eardley Holt in 1841. For reasons, which are not readily apparent, the following year, Bishop Sumner withdrew his licence for the performance of divine service at the house chapel and in 1842, Holt withdrew from Tilford leaving the villagers once more without a resident clergyman.

The Wares were away from Tilford for much of the time but kept in touch with these ministers to assess the needs of villagers and to offer help where necessary. Examples of the Ware's charitable works abound. "Although I may not be able often to visit Tilford, yet it will give Mrs Ware and myself pleasure to hear that everything is going on satisfactorily" writes Martin Ware in 1839 to the Reverend Dodds at Tilford "and should any of the deserving poor be in necessitous circumstances we shall be happy to contribute towards providing them with what may be necessary". This was no idle promise; numerous examples of their help in quiet unobtrusive ways both to individuals and to the villagers as a whole can be found. The Wares were very devout Christians, and Martin was most active in London where he was one of the founder members of the 'Ragged School Shoe Black Society' which sought to get children off the street into steady employment.

Contact with the village was maintained also through the tenants of Tilford House. Charlotte Smith, the well-known writer, stayed at the house in 1805 following the death of the previous tenant Mrs Munro. Crawford Davison occupied the house from 1813 to 1820, after which he moved to Pierrepont, subletting Tilford house first to Mr Bolero and then to the Reverend Ford. After Tayler's death in 1831, the Ware family (Martin and Anne and their five sons James, Martin, Charles, Joseph and Henry) occupied the house over the summer for three years. Whilst they were in Tilford, Martin commuted up to London from Tuesday to Saturday, travelling by post-chaise to Guildford and from there by coach to London. The strain of this was considerable, and after a bad attack of rheumatic fever in 1834, he decided to stay in London where the family had a house in Russell Square. Tilford House was again let, first to Dr Francis Burden, a retired physician and brother-in-law to Anne Ware's sister, and then to Major and Mrs Francklyn. After the Francklyns left in 1850, Martin then aged 61, returned with Anne to Tilford.

Anne Ware died in 1859, aged 67, and when Martin followed her in 1872, the estate passed to their son James who was unmarried. James decided to make Tilford House his home, and he took an active interest in managing the estate. He and his brothers were most solicitous in their appreciation of the best interests of the village and he was ably advised and assisted by them.

In 1836, Parliament passed the Tithe Commutation Act, which sought to replace the traditional but out-dated payments in kind to the Church by rent-charge equivalents. To establish this 'equivalence' it was necessary to apportion values to each plot of land and for this, accurate and

*34. Portrait of James Ware
(1817-1902)
(reproduced by permission of Surrey
History Service SHC 1576/37/5)*

James Ware, the owner of Tilford House, was a bachelor who, being the eldest son, inherited the property in 1878 from his father Martin Ware. When James died, he left the estate to his nephew Martin Stewart Ware.

comprehensive maps had to be drawn. The 'tithe-map' for Tilford was drawn up in 1840 and was accompanied by a 'tithe-apportionment' document, which listed all the plots, their areas and the uses to which they were put. This document and map allows us to make a thorough analysis of the village lands. Tilford was in the hands of three principal landowners: Ware of Tilford House, Stovold of Tilhill, and Nicholson of Waverley Abbey - who between them owned 84% of the allotted land; of this, over 50% was designated arable land.

Perhaps surprisingly, in view of the very strong emphasis on hop growing in Farnham itself, less than 3% of Tilford's land in 1840 was used for growing hops. This may have been due to constraints on the use of land and also, because the high prices commanded by Farnham hops were restricted to the small area around the centre of town, there was less incentive for the surrounding villages to focus on this crop. However, the demand for 'Farnham hops' continued to grow between 1840 and 1875 and exceeded the level that the centre of the town could supply. There was therefore increasing pressure on the surrounding villages to move more into hop-growing and there is considerable evidence to indicate that, after 1840, much of the Tilford was given over to hops and most, if not all, the farms in the village constructed hop kilns on their land.

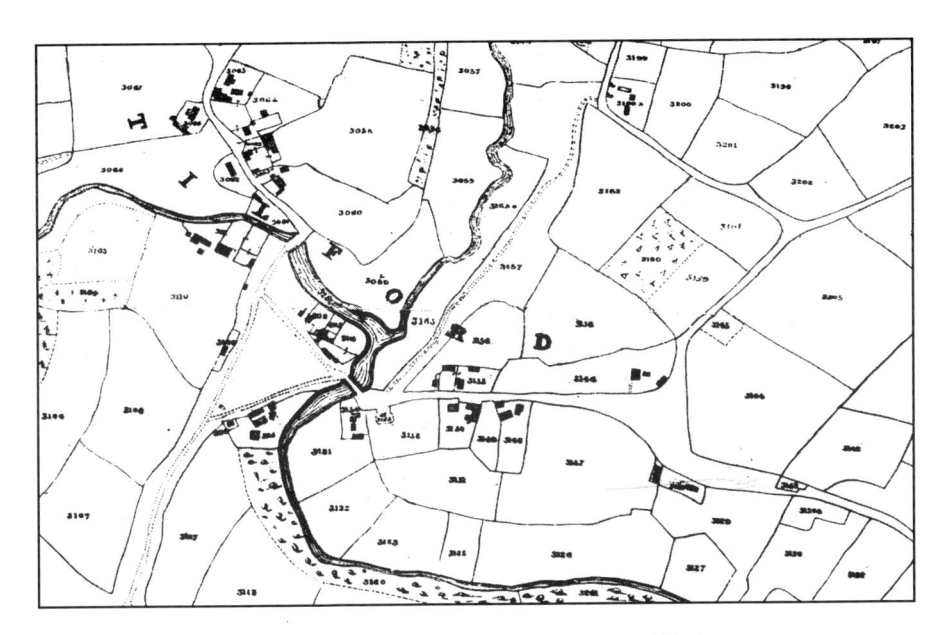

35. Part of the 1840 Tithe Map of Tilford
(reproduced by permission of Tilford Parish Council)

Under the Tithe Commutation Act of 1836, tithes were to be replaced by rent charge payments. Tithe Commissioners were set up to apportion the charges fairly, based on the land holdings of each tenant. The tithe map of Tilford was drawn up in 1840 by order of the Tithe Commissioners. Each plot was given a number, its area was measured, and its state of cultivation and value noted.

In 1841 Parliament authorised the first Population Census of Great Britain that listed individuals by name, age and occupation. Nation-wide censuses had been initiated in 1801, and repeated after every ten years, but these only gave overall figures - sufficient to yield an estimate of the population of Tilford but little else. The 1841 and subsequent censuses contain sufficient details for an assessment to be made of the character of the people living in Tilford. Over the fifty years from 1841 to 1891, Tilford's population steadily increased from 339 to 403, with the average age also increasing from twenty-one to twenty-eight or twenty-nine. At the start of the period, families in the village were overwhelmingly (77%) engaged in agriculture; but by 1891 this had fallen to under 50% reflecting the drastic changes that were occurring, and would continue to occur, in the character of the village. Figures for those born outside Farnham, who increased over the period from around 10 % to almost 40 %, illustrate the influx of those from outside the village seeking a 'life in the country'. Of interest, too, is the reduction in the numbers of children and the increase in the numbers of the elderly. Whilst the latter can easily be ascribed to the improved health and sanitary conditions achieved in Victorian times, the decrease in the percentage of youngsters in the village is not so easily interpreted. The increase in average age of the population is both a cause and effect of fewer youngsters, and it could be that young families were being displaced by older immigrants; alternatively it could be a reflection of a lower birth rate.

```
                COACHES.
LONDON from Southampton, The Times, arrives
     at the Bush Inn, at 12 o'clock daily.
LONDON from Southampton, through Guildford,
     The Red Rover, arrives at the Lion and
     Lamb Inn at 2 o'clock daily.
LONDON from Southampton, The Night Coach,
     arrives at Farnham at 2 o'clock in the
     morning.
LONDON from Gosport, The Express, arrives at
     the Lion and Lamb Inn at 1 o'clock daily.
LONDON from Alton, arrives at the Coffee House
     at half-past 9 every Monday, Wednesday,
     and Friday morning.
SOUTHAMPTON from London, The Times, ar-
     rives at the Bush Inn, at 12 o'clock daily.
SOUTHAMPTON from London, The Night Coach,
     arrives at the Lion and Lamb Inn, at 11
     o'clock every night.
GOSPORT from London, The Express, arrives at
     the Lion and Lamb Inn, at 1 o'clock daily.
ALTON from London, arrives at the Coffee House,
     at 4 o'clock every Tuesday, Thursday, and
     Saturday afternoon.
OXFORD from Brighton, The Hero, arrives at the
     Goat's Head Inn, every Tuesday, Thurs-
     day, and Saturday, and returns the follow-
     day at 1 o'clock.
FARNHAM to London, The Magnet, leaves Farn-
     ham every Monday, Wednesday, and Sa-
     turday morning, during the summer months,
     at ½ past 6 o'clock, leaves London at ½ past
     3, & arrives at Farnham at 8 the same day.
FRIMLEY & BLACKWATER to London, from
     the King's Arms, Blackwater, every morn-
     ing at 8 o'clock.
     None of the above Coaches run on Sunday.
```

36. Farnham Coach Timetable 1837 (from the Farnham Almanac for 1837, published by T. Fraser, Farnham)

Coaches through Farnham in the 19th century all ran to and from London except ' The Hero' which plied between Oxford and Brighton. In 1838, the railway reached Farnborough and coaches then went regularly from Farnham to meet the trains there. Eleven years later, the railway line had advanced to Farnham and the day's of long-distance horse-drawn coach journeys through the town were numbered.

Much of this change in the shape of Tilford can be directly ascribed to the advent of the railway which reached Farnham in 1849 and which brought London within striking distance of commuters and those seeking a haven in the country. Previously to this, travel to London was principally by coach - a very uncomfortable method with speeds rarely exceeding ten miles per hour even on the turnpikes. There was one cross-country route from Oxford to Brighton, otherwise all coaches ran to and from London. In

1838, the railway from London reached Farnborough and coaches ran to there from Farnham to enable passengers to take advantage of this link. An important domestic effect of the arrival of the railway was the delivery of coal. Previously to this, the main fuel for heating in Tilford's farmhouses and cottages had been turves from the commons or peat from the marshes near the river. The enclosure of the commons in 1853 stopped this source of supply. Grates suitable for coals were provided for the cottagers by their landlords and arrangements were made to help them in getting coals to supply the place of turves.

37. The Red Rover Coach plying between London and Southampton via Farnham 1837 (from 'Remembrances of Life and Customs in Gilbert White's, Cobbett's and Charles Kingsley's Country' by J. A. Eggar, published in 1924 by F. Sturt Ltd. Farnham)

On the unmetalled roads of the time, journeys by couch were most uncomfortable. Once the railways arrived, coaches took fewer and fewer passengers, the turnpike trusts lost income, and roads deteriorated further. It was not until 1883, when the burden of main road and bridge repairs devolved to the newly-created county councils, that the roads improved.

Travel around the village and to and from Farnham presented particular difficulties. The principal farmer in Tilford, Henry Harris of Tilford House Farm, was around this time made Surveyor of the Roads for the Parish and used his power to get a good part of the Farnham Road metalled, but it was full of ruts, and the road north of the Bourne water course up the last mile was a mere bed of sand through which carriages and passengers ploughed their way with great difficulty as best they could. The river Wey at Sheephatch was negotiable only by ford or by a plank footbridge, and the roads beyond Tilford were nothing more than tracks across the commons.

The track that turns off the Tilford to Churt road at Stonehills and passes by Stockbridge Pond was, before the 1853 enclosure, the main road from Tilford to Elstead.

38. The Plank Bridge at Sheephatch around 1870 showing 'Ellis's Lodge', one of the gateways to Waverley Abbey Estate.
(reproduced by permission of Surrey History Service SHC 1576/48/1)

Through the initiative of Thomas Darnley Anderson, owner of Waverley Abbey, a road bridge across the Wey at Sheephatch was constructed in 1876. Before that, the river at this point could only be crossed by ford or plank footbridge.

In his memoirs, Charles Ware speaks of when his father and mother (Martin and Anne Ware) used to visit Crawford Davison and his family at Pierrepont, "they turned off from what is now the Frensham Lane by the rough road to the left near the top of the hill and went by it through the narrow lane at the side of Reeds cottages up the steep bank to Tankersford Common across which they went by the 'Duke's Drive' a mere grass track across the Common - said to have been made or smoothed by the Duke of Kingston when owner of Pierrepont. The rest was a mere rough country lane with no main road at all - full of ruts and rough ground." He concludes: "Yet I suppose it was used by the Duke with his great equipage and was the best way of getting to Pierrepont." Anyone traversing this track today will appreciate that if this was 'the best way', the other so-called roads must have been indescribably bad.

Although the advent of the railway was the trigger for the changes that were to come in Tilford, it is unlikely that the far-reaching alteration in the whole structure of the village that occurred could have been achieved without the enclosure of the waste land that took place as a result of the Tilford Inclosure Award of 1853. Although the acquisition of the waste under this award was initially inspired by a move to increase agricultural output, the effect in Tilford and in many other places in Surrey, was to bring common land (which was often of only marginal agricultural use) into private ownership and encourage the development of 'country residences' for wealthy outsiders - a process commonly described as 'gentrification'. The waste land in Tilford covered almost 1,300 acres and was greater in extent than all of the allotted land. It extended over Crooksbury Common in the east, Abbots Plain in the south, Tancredsford Common in the west, and Boundstone Common in the northwest. Land from the waste was allotted to landowners broadly in proportion to their existing holdings and had to be fenced in. Much discussion and debate took place before decisions were made and the process took several years to complete. As a result, the landowners enhanced the area and value of their properties whilst the dispossessed lost their rights to grazing, turbary and estovers on what had previously been common land.

After the enclosures the land holding remained, as before, in the hands of three main owners: Ware, Stovold and Nicholson - a distribution that was to remain in place until well into the 20th century. For such owners, the enclosure proved to be a source of much wealth, with land being sought by developers bringing in good returns. In addition, the hop trade, which took off in Tilford in the second half of the nineteenth century, had brought increased income to the farmers. Landowners started to rebuild their houses; Henry Mansell of Squires Hill Farm, replaced his farmhouse (now Wey Cottage) around 1860 and around the same time, Thomas Stovold showed off his new wealth by building Tilhill House alongside his farm, where he could lord it on the east side of the river like Martin Ware was able to do on the west. Ware himself had not been tardy. Chapel farmhouse had been completely rebuilt on its new site in 1836/37 and his other properties were thoroughly renovated in 1841.

One of the earliest examples of 'development', taking advantage of the additional land released by enclosure, was the erection of a cottage, probably built as two dwellings, on the waste at Charles Hill next to the

Elstead boundary. The cottage was acquired by George Trimmer in 1864 (who had set up the Lion Brewery in Farnham ten years earlier) and converted into an alehouse which he named the 'Half-Way House' - later on to be renamed 'The Donkey'. Nearby, just across the border into Elstead, was Absalom Harris's pottery works and this thirsty business must have provided much custom for the new pub in addition to that of the travellers from Elstead to Farnham and Tilford who would have appreciated the welcome half-way stop.

On the other side of Tilford, in the 1850's, another new inn was built on the edge of what was Abbots Pond, which had broken its banks in 1841 following a particularly violent November gale. Created in 1250 by the monks of Waverley Abbey for stocking fish, Abbots Pond was a profitable bit of property and Mr Prichard, the owner of Pitfold Manor, who bought the pond in 1831, could not have been very pleased when he was told on that blustery November day in 1841 that his assets had disappeared. He sold off the land the next year and a house was built by its new owner on its northern edge. In 1858, the property was bought by 'grocer and farmer' Henry Caesar who, in his new capacity as 'farmer and beer retailer', developed the building as a Public House. Some 20 years on, capitalising on the popularity of the Duke of Cambridge after the Crimean War, the duke's famous name was adopted as the sign of the house. It has recently been renamed 'The Hankley'.

Another developer to take advantage of the land released in Tilford by the 1853 enclosure was William Hazell who, straight away, purchased the land allocated to Thomas Stovold lying to the east of the newly-constructed Tilford-Churt road next-door to the Tilford-Frensham boundary. In 1857, Miss Elizabeth Strickland acquired this $4^{1}/_{2}$-acre plot from Hazell and built a house on the northern half. Taking the name from the now defunct Abbots Pond, she called it Abbots Lodge, a name that is retained to this day. In 1876, following the death of Elizabeth, the property reverted to her sister Sarah who built a cottage, called South Bank Cottage, on the southern half of the plot. Now called Gorse Cottage, the residence assumed fame nine years later when it was let to Henry Salt. Henry was a Humanitarian reformer and man of letters who taught at Eton. In 1885 he decided that he and his wife Kate would retire to a 'tiny cottage in the wilds of Surrey, where he hoped he would be free from intrusion'.

39. Henry and Kate Salt at South Bank Cottage (Gorse Cottage) Tilford c.1890

(reproduced by kind permission of Miss Anthea How, Gorse Cottage, Tilford)

George Bernard Shaw was one of many well-known people who visited Henry and Kate Salt whilst they lived at Southbank Cottage from 1885 to 1891. After such a visit in 1888, GBS wrote an amusing 'tongue-in-cheek' article for the Pall Mall Gazzette of April 28th entitled 'A Sunday in the Surrey Hills' In it, he complains that Salt "keeps a house in a hole called Tilford down Farnham way". He clearly has little time for the attractions of the countryside.

This was not to be. Many of his friends and colleagues travelled down to Tilford to see him: Edward Carpenter, William Morris, John Burns, George Meredith, G.K.Chesterton, Sydney Webb and Beatrice Potter, and George Bernard Shaw being amongst them. In an article in the Pall Mall Gazette of April 28th 1888 Shaw describes his visit to Tilford and Salt in a satirical vein. "I allowed myself to be persuaded" he said "by my friend S--- and his wife to 'come down and stay until Monday' among the Surrey Hills. S---, a man of exceptional intelligence on most subjects, is country mad and keeps a house at a hole called Tilford down Farnham way". Reaching Farnham by train, he walks all the way to Tilford in the pouring rain. Having reached there he finds he has to go "up another hill between meeting house and church and out upon an exposed section of road where the wind and rain had an unobstructed final pelt at me." He finally reaches Gorse Cottage soaking wet and in a bad frame of mind!

Others were keen to take advantage of the access provided by the Tilford-Churt road, and Greenhills, Greenhill Farm, and Stockbridge Cottages were also built on land released by the enclosures. Elsewhere in the village, similar developments were occurring and 'notables' were moving in to build mansions out of the town. In 1883, The Barrows at Charles Hill was built for Frank Mangles JP followed shortly afterwards by Riversleigh for Mrs Marshall.

In Crooksbury, part of the enclosed land to the east of the Elstead-Farnham road was bought in 1888/89 by Arthur Chapman JP and Coldham Crump Knight for their houses, Crooksbury House (designed by Lutyens) and Monk's Hill. Knight was a descendant of the Coldhams who owned Waverley Abbey and a relative of John Knight who achieved fame and fortune in Farnham as an inventor and entrepreneur. In 1886, Colonel John Davis acquired Whitmead. Normanswood was built by Dr Field in 1894 and Squires Hill House by Rupert Anderson of Waverley Abbey, in the same year. The rush to the country had begun.

40. Domestic Staff at 'The Barrows' c.1900
(reproduced by kind permission of the Thomas Family Archives)

Built in 1883 at Charles Hill Tilford by Frank Mangles J.P. and named after the five Bronze Age 'barrows' in the grounds of the house.

The enclosure also gave to the village the triangular green as a place of recreation and also three plots of land at Charles Hill, Crooksbury, and Stockbridge as 'allotments for the labouring poor'. These areas in Tilford were placed in the charge of the Parish Churchwardens and Overseers of the Poor whose responsibilities, in the course of time, devolved on to Tilford Parish Council.

The enclosure of land in Tilford in 1853 not only brought the waste into private ownership it also was responsible for the laying down of new roads and the re-organisation of the existing tracks in and around the village. Fifteen track roads were compulsorily discontinued and 2 public roads and 19 private roads were authorised. The two new public roads were from the West Bridge southwards to the boundary (at what would become Grange Road) and from the existing track off the Tilford-Farnham Road westwards to the boundary at the Reeds. At last, there was a proper road southwards from Tilford which, connecting with a similar new road authorised for Frensham, (which led eventually to the developement of Rushmoor) enabled traffic through Tilford to reach the London-Portsmouth turnpike.

The change in the road layout and the closure of many of the village tracks together with the obligation on the new owners to fence in their enclosed land led to marked changes in the landscape. Whilst the enclosed land had originally been intended for agriculture, its poor quality led the land holders to think of different ways of using it. Many considered forestry to be a profitable venture. Sir Robert Rich had led the way in the previous century when he planted Crooksbury Hill with Scotch firs; and his successors at Waverley Abbey had followed suit in both Crooksbury and on Boundstone Common along the Farnham Road. Other landowners decided to copy this initiative and soon, more and more of the heath had been converted to coniferous forest. Whilst the commons remained open, young seedlings had been cut off with the turves dug out by the villagers and the commons remained bare. After enclosure, great quantities of young firs sprang up producing extensive woods that spread over a large part of the erstwhile commons. The landscape was changed for good and 'the beauty of the wide heaths and many glorious distant views from the high ground were interrupted by the trees.' In his memoirs, Charles Ware laments in particular the loss of "the splendid views towards Hindhead which the road from Farnham to Godalming over Charles Hill running like a terrace across the high ground under Crooksbury Hill."

Enclosure had to have the consent of the principal landowners and at first, Martin Ware was not favourable to enclosure of the commons. In his memoirs, Martin Ware's son, Charles, recalls: "my father was reluctant to consent to an enclosure, thinking it would be injurious to the cottagers, depriving them of their fuel and interfering with their commonage for animals - besides altering the character of the place." However, events caused him to change his mind. Charles continues: "Some of the people of Farnham had got into the way of coming on to the Tilford Commons cutting and carrying off the turves to burn for manure for hop grounds. On one occasion, some of the Farnham people had come with waggons to carry off some of the turves when Mr Crawford Davison of Pierrepont assembled some of the Tilford men and a fight ensued, with the result that the Farnham men were driven away and the victors took the waggons to the green and distributed the turves among the cottagers. After this my father saw that the time had come for an enclosure and consented to it." Charles Ware concludes by adding: "Before the enclosure there was occasionally some difficulty in the men getting work but the great demand for labour caused by the enclosure in the way of road making, fencing, and bringing newly-enclosed land into cultivation etc was such that from that time no man ever failed to get regular work who cared to do it. I believe that unquestionably the enclosure improved the condition of the working classes."

41. *Harvesting Scene, rear of Tilford House, 1850's*
(reproduced by kind permission of the Old Kiln Museum Trust, Tilford)

This was not the opinion of George Sturt who wrote (under the pseudonym Bourne) in his book 'Change in the Village' about how the enclosure had affected Bourne (to the northwest of Tilford) in the late nineteenth century. Deploring the loss of the 'yeoman farmer', he points to the influx of the new 'immigrant' employers who saw themselves as set apart from their working class labouring employees, whose self-esteem suffered as a consequence. Whilst this might have applied to the Bourne, the conditions described by Sturt did not, however, have such a marked effect on Tilford where the Wares, the Davisons, and the Nicholsons, living in their grand houses and often away from the village, had always been a group apart. Their wealth allowed them to rise above 'class warfare' and indeed, they used that wealth to provide much needed help and philanthropy in the village.

In Tilford, whilst there were no children 'on the street', nevertheless with little to amuse them and school to be avoided wherever possible, the village youngsters were 'a wild lot' and 'Tilford was a very rough place'. It was not until 1851 that a police force was set up in Surrey and, four years later, a resident policeman, PC Peter Collett, was appointed in Tilford.

42. Fire Practice on Tilford Green 1897
(reproduced by kind permission of the Museum of Farnham owner of the copyright)

The Merryweather 'Steamer' christened Victoria in honour of the Queen in 1896 was regularly exercised at Tilford where there was space on the Green and a plentiful supply of water. A pair of horses pulled the engine and a buglar on a bicycle was sent in advance to alert the village to the forthcoming display.

At first, the turn-over was frequent. Many of those appointed were dismissed the service for offences such as 'frequenting public houses' or larceny and replacements often lasted no more than a year each. This went on until PC William Finch was appointed in 1865; he was accommodated in No 3 Stockbridge Cottages and remained in Tilford until 1878 and proved to be a very good officer. Twenty years later, another popular police officer appointed to Tilford, PC George Sumner, was presented with a gift of £11 from the inhabitants of the village to mark his retirement after 24 years of active service in the police force.

Another force with strong connections with Tilford was the fire service. The Vestry in Farnham had taken on responsibility for this around 1835 but had transferred such responsibility to a newly formed Local Board in 1866. Tilford came under their aegis but until 1896, calls on the fire service from the village go unrecorded. However, in that year, Waverley mill caught fire and the fire brigade with its new steam fire engine which had been inaugurated only the day before, was called out to deal with it. Unhappily, such was the state of the road and the difficulty in dealing with the horses, that by the time the brigade reached Waverley, the mill had been completely gutted. Tilford thus lost the last of its three mills, and one which had operated continuously since the middle ages when it had been built by the monks of Waverley Abbey.

43. Waverley Abbey Mill c. 1890
(reproduced by kind permission of the Museum of Farnham owner of the copyright)

Waverley Abbey Mill shown on the right of the picture was one of three fulling/corn mills in Tilford. It suffered a disastrous fire in November 1896 from which it never recovered; the building was demolished around 1900.

The apportionment of the tithes in Farnham not only led to a more clearly defined rent-charge for the church authorities it also led to calls for this money to be reallocated so that outside villages, such as Tilford, could benefit more directly. Traditionally, tithes had been allocated to the Archdeacon of Surrey for him to dispense to the parishes as he thought fit. In 1840, alongside the tithe-apportionment proposals, the Bishop of Winchester had published a Bill to be debated in Parliament which sought to take away this means of collection in Farnham and allocate the tithes directly to new benefices. The plan was to divide the Farnham tithes into five parts with two going to Farnham town, and one each to Tilford, Hale and Wrecclesham so that there would be separate rectories in each. The Bill did not succeed in Parliament but the idea lived on, causing much discussion and controversy in the parish.

In the end, although Tilford did not get its guaranteed benefit of one-fifth of the tithes, there was pressure to fulfil the aim in the bishop's Bill to constitute Tilford 'a separate District for Ecclesiastical Purposes' and the 1853 Inclosure Award provided an opportunity for this to be achieved. A site of 10 acres was to be set aside for a church, parsonage and school at Stonehills.

44. All Saints' School Tilford c. 1870
(reproduced from the Ware family album 31.40 by kind permission of the Old Kiln Museum Trust, Tilford)

Constructed in 1857 and used as a church for ten years until 1867 when All Saints Church was consecrated, Tilford's first purpose-built school was enlarged in 1879. Two new classrooms were opened this July.

Although this was the nearest parcel of waste to the centre of the village, there was much concern that it remained too far out and Martin Ware agreed to exchange this plot for four acres alongside the village green. Initially, the bishop wanted a square plot covering what is now All Saints School and the vicarage and extending into the woods behind, but eventually settled for the rectangular shape the school/church complex now occupies. In 1856 a committee was formed to raise money for the project and later on that year subscriptions were sought from the public. The following year the first building was erected on the site. Although destined eventually to be a school, the building was used temporarily for religious services whilst All Saints Church was being built. At the other end of the plot, a burial ground was established and consecrated on 28th March 1858.

A key date in Tilford's history is 30th November 1865 when an Order in Council established Tilford as a separate Ecclesiastical District. Up to this date, Tilford had been served by a curate from St Andrews in Farnham; it now had a permanent incumbent, the Reverend W T Jones. The exchange of letters between Jones, Utterton (the Vicar of St Andrews), and Ware reveals much concern over where Jones was to live and what stipend he would receive. In the nick of time sufficient funding was raised though a combination of donors and Jones was temporarily accommodated at Heathyfield (now Sheephatch House) until the parsonage was built. Under Ewan Christian as the architect, work started on All Saints Church in 1866

45. All Saints' Church and Parsonage c. 1880
(reproduced by kind permission of the Thomas Family Archives)

All Saint's church was built in 1867 and the Parsonage in 1868. In 1898 the church was enlarged by the addition of a south aisle, and 1904 and 1956 saw extensions to the churchyard. A new vicarage was built in 1967 to replace the Parsonage, which was sold into private hands.

and on the 27th of July the foundation stone was laid by Martin Ware. The contract for building the church was £1,650 and that for the parsonage £2,000; these, together with a further £350 for incidentals, amounted to £4,000. By 1867, contributions had reached £2,930 and a mortgage of £700 had been secured. The fund-raising committee were confident that they could meet the deficiency of £370 and pressed ahead. Their confidence was rewarded by the church's consecration on 10th of July that year, followed by completion of the parsonage in 1868.

Following on the consecration of All Saints, the building erected in 1857 and meanwhile used as a temporary church, reverted to its original design function as a school. This was not the first school in Tilford. In the early 1830's Mrs Anne Ware had promoted a 'Dame School' under Eliza Eade in the cottage next to the Barley Mow where she lived with her widowed mother Mary. Sunday School was run by Charlotte Eade, her cousin, who had endeared herself to Anne when they had both listened to an open-air Preacher on the Green. She was, according to Anne's son, Charles Ware,

46. Tilford's First Village School (No 1 Tilford Green Cottages) in the 1850's. ('Dame' Eade speaking to Mrs Anne Ware).
(reproduced from the Ware family album 31.28 by kind permission of the Old Kiln Museum Trust, Tilford)

The school mistress, Eliza Eade, known as 'Dame' Eade, lived with her mother Mary and three other relations in the cottage used as the village school which was next to the Barley Mow Public House. The picture shown Dame Eade at the gate talking with Mrs Anne Ware with two of her 30 pupils standing nearby. Sadly, it was not long after this photograph was taken that Mrs Ware had a stroke and died in the schoolhouse.

"the only person whom she could find in Tilford that thoroughly sympathised with her in religious things". The Wares were wholly supportive of both day and Sunday schools. Around thirty children from the village attended the day school (for which the charge was 6 pence a week) and of these, twenty were funded by Anne Ware. Mrs Ware also paid Charlotte Eade an annual salary of £6.6s.0d. for her Sunday School work. In 1850, following another round of fund-raising, the chapel by the Green was extended by the addition of a schoolroom, which on Sundays housed some 40 children for religious instruction.

Meanwhile, Tilford had to wait until the church had been constructed before the purpose-built All Saints School could open its doors to pupils. Eliza Eade had reached 61 by this time and when her school yielded up its pupils to the new establishment, some 50 children, ranging in age from 3 to 14, attended in the summer of 1867. Parents paid for their children's education according to their means - from a penny to three-pence per week. Elizabeth Wheeler took over as head teacher, assisted by various pupil-teachers, and the subjects taught ranged over the traditional subjects of arithmetic, grammar, writing, poetry, singing, scripture, catechism, history, and geography with needlework for the girls and drill, marching, and gardening for the boys.

The school timetable revolved around the farming year with the four-weeks so-called 'hopping break' extending from August/September to September/October. Children were often away from school because of the

47. Tilford's famous cricketer
William 'Silver Billy' Beldham aged 84.
(reproduced by kind permission of the Curator, Lords Cricket Ground, St John's Wood, London, NW8)

William Beldham was born in Wrecclesham in 1766. A farmer by trade, he came to Tilford in 1821 when he took over as landlord of the Barley Mow Public House.
He died in Tilford in 1862 and is buried in Tilford Churchyard.

demands of hop-picking, or helping at home, or illness, or from other, more agreeable activities, such as watching the soldiers exercise on the village green or visiting Farnham Fair. To begin with, the school progressed very well, but following successive yearly changes of head-teachers after Elizabeth Wheeler left in 1869, standards took a down-turn and it was some time before the School Inspectors were able again to commend the school's performance as highly as in their first few reports.

Towards the end of the century there was much discussion over how best to provide recreational facilities for the villagers. The Green which had been reserved for this purpose had promoted much interest in cricket and this had been greatly stimulated, earlier on, by the arrival in the village of Surrey's most famous cricketer, 'Silver Billy' Beldham. Beldham was a legend in his own time, playing for the famous Hambledon club. He played his last major game at Lords in 1821 when he was 55 years old and in the same year he and his family moved to Tilford where he took over as landlord of the Barley Mow Public House. His impact on Tilford cricket can be imagined and much has been written on his feats and prowess on Tilford Green. In the 1840's he built a cottage next to Tilford Oak to house himself and his son-in-law, William Caesar, the village blacksmith. Originally a single-storey building known as 'Beldams Cottage' (*sic*), it was later (1870) given a second storey and renamed 'Oak Cottage'.

The village had its own Drum and Fife band and a number of clubs brought villagers together, but apart from the Barley Mow, the Half-way House and the Duke of Cambridge, the only places where the villagers could congregate were the church or the chapel. What was needed was a meeting house or village hall where recreational facilities could be provided. Much thought was given, particularly by the leading personalities in the village, to how this might best be achieved. As early as 1877, John Davis, who was renting the lands at Greenhills, wrote to James Ware from his London home suggesting that the chapel on the Green might be converted to a meeting and reading room so that his servants "could be more independent of the beer house". The chapel had had a declining attendance for some time and discussions were proceeding as to its future role. The last service was held in the chapel in 1888. Five years of lengthy discussions between Ware and the Surrey Mission Society (SMS) ensued before agreement was reached in 1893 and the Charity Commission was able to authorise the sale of the chapel to a new set of trustees.

48. *Tilford's Drum and Fife Band c.1900*
(reproduced by kind permission of the Old Kiln Museum Trust, Tilford)

Tilford's Drum and Fife band played an active part in Tilford's social life in the late 19th century. The bass drum, which was its prize possession, is now on show at the Rural Life Centre, Tilford.

Events then moved more rapidly. A committee was formed and subscriptions were sought; Edwin Lutyens was commissioned to prepare drawings and a figure of £418 was estimated for the cost. At first, the level of subscriptions was disappointing and only £118 remained after deducting the purchase price of £120, which had been agreed with the SMS. However, thanks to the generosity of the Anderson family who had succeeded Nicholson at Waverley Abbey in 1870, more money became available and soon over £500 was on the table. This was now more than that needed for the conversion, so it was decided to proceed with a grander scheme and to build a brand-new Institute - to cost well on a £1,000. James Ware agreed to exchange land which he owned on the opposite side of the road with that on which the chapel stood. The chapel was demolished and its masonry used as foundations for the new, Lutyens-designed, Institute. Work got underway quickly, galvanised by Charles Anderson who had taken a strong personal interest in the project. Tragically, in November 1893, Charles, then only 44 years of age, died suddenly leaving a grief-stricken widowed mother, Dorothy. She decided to undertake all further expenses of the Institute and to dedicate it to the memory of her son.

49. Tilford's Oldest Inn, the 'Barley Mow', c.1900's
(reproduced by kind permission of Mr Geoff Dye)

The Barley Mow Inn at Tilford was built in the early 18th century as an extension of the cottage next door, which itself was built in 1601.

The Institute was completed in 1894 and opened two days after Christmas to a celebration which embraced all of the village. It was an immediate success with frequent 'entertainments', concerts, lectures, and theatrical performances arranged. Billiards became very popular, a Mothers Union was formed with nearly 60 members, and the Cricket Club used it as their clubhouse. As if encouraged by this, Richard Combe, who in 1862 had taken over Pierrepont from Crawford Davison, and the Vicar of Churt, the Reverend Augustus Watson, got together in November 1896 to found the Hankley Common Golf Club. A nine-hole course was laid out on Hankley Common and a room at the Duke of Cambridge was designated the clubhouse.

The end of the century was marked by requests for money. In 1879, H.M. Inspector of Schools had declared that the village school needed enlarging and in spite of it being vested in Farnham parish, Tilford was called upon to subscribe over £300 to pay for it. Meanwhile there were fresh requests for money by the church. At this time, the parish of Tilford included the lower part of the Bourne which was cut off from Tilford both by distance and by difficulty of access. The inhabitants there needed their own place of worship and in 1887, two ladies living there put up the money to buy the land for a Mission Church.

50. Tilford Institute

Designed by Sir Edwin Lutyens, the Institue at Tilford is situated on the Village Green next-door to All Saints School. It was built in 1894, extended in 1965, and enlarged in 1998.

In the face of yet another demand for money, the people of Tilford initially refused to support the venture. They had another fund-raising initiative to contend with. Increasing numbers attending All Saints' church had led the vicar, the Reverend Edge, to look to its possible enlargement. Donations were called for and led by a gift of £250 from Colonel Davis, the total by 1898 had reached close on £1,200. With an estimate of £1,332 from the builder, Martin Wells of Aldershot, it was decided to go ahead, and Edwin Lutyens was approached to prepare plans for the enlargement. His design, however, was not in the end accepted and it was under J. H. Christian as architect, that All Saints acquired a new south aisle, vestry, and heating. The Mission Church had to wait its turn and it was not until 1903 that sufficient funding was realised to meet the cost of over £1,000 needed to build and furnish it.

Ironically, just as the church was expanding its facilities in Tilford, it was losing its long-standing administrative function. The year 1894 saw the coming into force of the Local Government Act, which transferred powers from the Church Vestry to Parish Councils and set up Rural District Councils.

NOTICE OF PARISH MEETING.

Tilford Ward of the Parish of Farnham Rural.

1. Notice is hereby given that the first Parish Meeting for the above-named Ward will be held at the National Schools, Tilford, on Tuesday, the Fourth day of December, One thousand eight hundred and ninety-four, at Six o'clock in the evening.

2. The business to be transacted at the Meeting will be as follows:—
   (a) **To elect a Chairman for the Meeting.**
   (b) **To elect Parish Councillors.**

3. The number of Parish Councillors to be elected at the Meeting is 2.

4. Each candidate for election as a Parish Councillor must be nominated in writing, and the nomination paper must be handed in at the Parish Meeting.

5. A parochial elector may sign 2 nomination papers, but no more.
   A parochial elector must not sign a nomination paper for more than one Ward or for a Ward for which he is not registered in respect of a qualification in that Ward.

6. Forms of nomination paper may be obtained, free of charge, from us at the Office of the Assistant Overseer, Mr. A. J. NASH, South Street, Farnham.

7. The nomination paper must be in the following form or in a form to the like effect:—

FORM OF NOMINATION PAPER.

Election of Parish Councillors for the Tilford Ward of the Parish of Farnham Rural, in the year 1894.

We, the undersigned, being respectively parochial electors of the said Ward do hereby nominate the under-mentioned person as a candidate at the said Election.

Names of Candidates		Place of Abode.	Description.	Whether qualified as Parochial Elector or by Residence
Surname	Other Names in full			
1	2	3	4	5

Signature of Proposer
Place of Abode
Signature of Seconder
Place of Abode

Instructions for filling up Nomination Paper.

1. The surname of only one candidate for election must be inserted in Column 1.
2. The other names of the candidate must be inserted in full in Column 2.
3. Insert in Column 3 the place of abode of the candidate.
4. In Column 4 state the occupation, if any, of the candidate. If the candidate has no occupation insert some such description as "gentleman," or "married woman," or "spinster," or "widow," as the case may be.
5. If the candidate is a parochial elector of the Parish (that is, if his or her name is registered in the register of parochial electors of the Parish) insert in Column 5 "Parochial Elector." If the candidate is not a parochial elector of the Parish, but he or she has, during the twelve months preceding the election, resided in the Parish or within three miles of it, insert in Column 5 "Residence." If the candidate is a parochial elector of the Parish and has also, during the whole of the twelve months preceding the election, resided in the Parish or within three miles of it, it will be sufficient to insert in Column 5 either "Parochial Elector" or "Residence," but both may be inserted.
6. The paper must be signed by two parochial electors of the Ward and no more, by one as proposer, and by the other as seconder. The places of abode of the Proposer and Seconder must also be inserted.

DATED this Twentieth day of November, One thousand eight hundred and ninety-four.

George H. Bracewell
Henry Patrick } *Overseers.*
Charles Smith

51. Notice of First Parish Meetiing at Tilford 4th December 1894.
(reproduced by permission of Tilford Parish Council)

The Parish of Farnham Rural was formed under the Local Government Act of 1894, with Tilford as one of its Wards. Its resonsibilities were inherited by Tilford Parish Council in 1933.

Tilford became one of the three constituent members of Farnham Rural District, the other two being Hale and Wrecclesham. From this time on, the inhabitants of Tilford were able to elect councillors to represent them and the days of paternalism were over.

Chapter 12

Progress and Plenty

The twentieth century was a time of accelerating change in Tilford. The once exclusively farming community is turned into a dormitory village where half the adult population are 'economically inactive', and most of those in work are in jobs outside the area. As large-scale agriculture became more efficient, there was little room for the smaller farms of yester-year and the estates in Tilford, which had been built up in the nineteenth century, became increasingly unprofitable and were sold off to developers. Today,

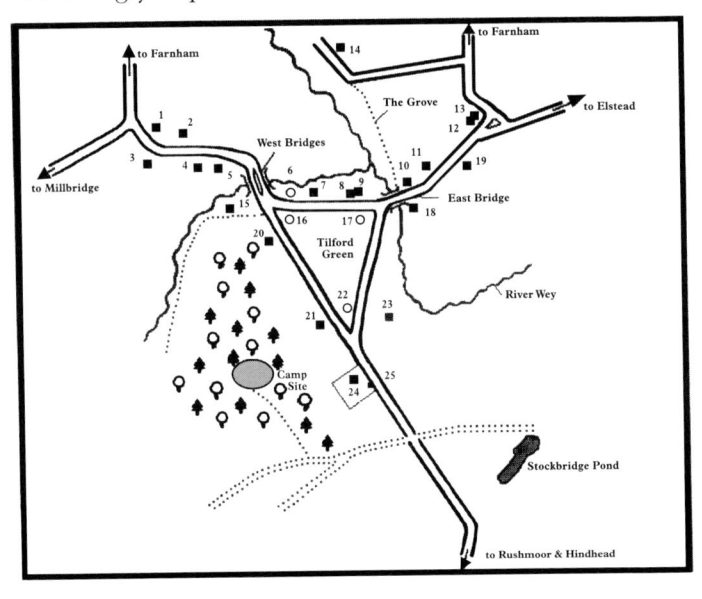

Legend:
1. Tilford House Farm   2. Tilford House   3. Beagley's Cottages   4. Tilford Cottage
5. Bridge Cottage   6. Tilford Oak   7. Oak Cottage   8. Barley Mow PH
9. Tilford Green Cottages   10. Post Office & Garage   11. Street Farm   12. Woodhill Farm
13. Caesar's Corner   14. Tilhill House   15. The Malthouse
16. King Edward VII Coronation Oak   17. Queen Victoria Diamond Jubilee Oak
18. Bridge Farm   19. Upper Street Farm   20. Tilford Institute   21. All Saints' School
22. King George V Accession Oak   23 Chapel Farm House   24 All Saints' Church
25. Tilford War Memorial

52. Tilford Green and its Surroundings

farming has all but deserted the village. As roads improved and travel by motor vehicle became the norm, mobility vastly increased and work was no longer restricted to the local area. Modern means of communication, the telephone, television, and now the internet, have altered social patterns, and universal education has fundamentally changed political attitudes. Tilford, today, is a well-ordered, attractive, village community with many enviable facilities located in a 'green belt' area designated as one of 'outstanding natural beauty' and 'great landscape value'.

The start of the twentieth century saw Tilford blessed with a parish church barely 35 years old, a thriving school, three public houses and a brand-new Institute. The Post Office and shop, run by Elizabeth Tilbury and her children Willie and Annie, had been established in the 1850's and the telegraph had reached Tilford in 1898. That year, also, saw a cinematograph show laid on at the Institute which the newspapers described as 'a novelty for this village'. The Boer War ended in 1902, there was an optimistic spirit around, and Tilford was feeling buoyant.

53. James Novell, Tilford's oldest inhabitant, Planting the Queen Victoria Diamond Jubilee Oak Tree on Tilford Green 7th December 1897.

(reproduced by kind permission of the Thomas Family Archives)

The Planting of an oak tree in 1897 to celebrate Queen Victoria's Diamond Jubilee started a 'tradition' which has been maintained ever since. Tilford Green now has eight oak trees (including the famous Tilford Oak) commemorating memorable occasions.

Five years earlier, in 1897, the village marked Queen Victoria's Diamond Jubilee by planting an oak tree at the north-east corner of the green in front of the blacksmith's shop and this was followed in 1902 by a second oak tree at the north-west corner to mark King Edward VII's coronation. These two oaks complement the venerable old tree near the West Bridge, which has become one of the symbols of the village. Known variously as the King's Oak, Novell's Oak, Bishop's Oak, and Tilford Oak, it has been the subject of many tales. King Charles II is reputed to have hidden in its branches, a Waverley monk is said to have hanged himself from it, Queen Elizabeth I is reported to have dined or to have shot a stag under it, and John Wesley supposedly preached beneath it. William Cobbett noted that he saw it as a little boy (possibly when he accompanied his father when he made his survey of the Abney Estate in 1767) and also when he visited Tilford during one of his rural rides in 1822. Its age has been variously estimated at anything up to 1,000 years, although the latest view is that it was planted in the first half of the 17th century. Tilford Oak was in its prime

54. *Tilford Oak and Oak Cottage c.1860*
(*reproduced by kind permission of the Tilford Women's Institute*)

Tilford's famous oak was in its prime in the 19th century. Its age has been variously estimated at anything up to 1000 years. Oak Cottage to the west of Tilford Oak was built for William Beldham in 1841; a second storey was added in 1870.

in the 19th century. Since then, it has seen successive limbs chopped off one after another. The big bough that used to extend over the road was taken off around 1910, the inside was scraped out and dressed over with preservative and lead and zinc sheets were used to cover the cavity - and other similar surgery followed in the 1950's and 60's. Once described as the finest oak in Surrey, it is now, alas, only a shadow of its former self but with continued care there is hope that it will remain the pride of the village for a good many years to come.

In their capacity as Lords of the Manor, the various bishops of Winchester have had mixed views on Tilford Oak. In the eighteenth century the villagers drove spikes and nails into it to prevent the then bishop (known as money-loving Brownlow) from cutting it down and the then owner of Tilford House, Miss Elizabeth Abney, paid him £40 to leave the tree alone. In 1853, when the Green was handed over to the village under the Inclosure Act, the bishop again declared an interest and was effective in getting the oak and the area around it excluded from the award. It wasn't until 1950 that the Church Commissioners acting for the bishop released the tree and the land into the care of the Parish Council.

55. Mary Ware (1834-1914), the widowed mother of Martin Stewart Ware, the owner of Tilford House, being presented with a basket of roses by Norman Lonsdale in 1911 after planting the oak tree at Tilford to commemorate the coronation of George V.
(reproduced by permission of Surrey History Service SHC 1576/39/3).

Following the accession of King George V[th] in 1911, the village decided to commemorate the occasion by a fourth oak. The site chosen was the southern corner of the Green and on June 22nd of that year, the oak, donated by R.D. Anderson JP, was planted by Mrs Mary Ware (mother of the Reverend Martin Stewart Ware) assisted by Norman Lonsdale, one of the youngest inhabitants of the village. Sadly, it blew down in the 1987 hurricane and a replacement had to be found. An acorn from the 1911 tree, which had been planted and tended by John Ewins from the village, was chosen as a fitting substitute - and, in 1988, his granddaughter, Sarah, undertook the task of planting it. Alas, like its parent tree, this one did not last the course and a third was planted in 1989 in its stead. This third oak was provided out of the Tilford Oaks fund that had been set up in the wake of the 1987 hurricane and to which both villagers and Surrey and Waverley Councils had contributed. The fund enabled extensive repairs and renovations to be made to the older trees - in particular the King Edward VII tree. The trunk of the KGV tree found a role in All Saints School playground where it acts as a challenging climbing frame!

Three other oaks adorn the Green: one planted in 1936 on the west side close by the bus shelter to commemorate the Coronation of King George VIth; one planted by the stone seat close to the river on the east side to mark the closing of Sheephatch school in 1977; and one to mark the Silver Jubilee of Queen Elizabeth in 1978 - planted alongside its venerable counterpart, the Tilford Oak.

In July 1894, the Local Government Act established Farnham Rural District which encompassed three wards: Tilford, Wrecclesham and Hale. On the fourth of December that year, the people of Tilford met at the school to elect two councillors to the new Rural District Council. Three in the village put their names forward: Major Henry Crofton Caldwell from Heathyfield (now Sheephatch House), Coldham Crump Knight, barrister, from Monk's Hill, and Sam Poulter, farmer, from Street Farm. It soon became clear that Sam Poulter was the popular choice amongst those attending. He secured 58 votes, Caldwell 45 and Knight 25. Knight thereupon demanded a poll. This was held on December 17th with the result that Poulter received 110, Crofton 71 and Knight 64 votes. For the first time in the Tilford's history, the villagers had elected representatives to speak for them in local government.

Their first complaint, and one which was to continue to echo down the years, was the danger of crossing the roads. A resolution was passed 'that several accidents having nearly taken place at the Tilford Bridges the Parish meeting wishes to urge upon the Parish Council the necessity of having them properly lighted during the winter months'. Needless to say, no action resulted, and apart from a request to 'cleanse the bed of the river Wey' raised on a subsequent occasion, the Annual Parish Meetings at Tilford were the source of nothing but the election of representative to the Farnham Rural District Council for umpteen years to come.

56. Mr Willie Tilbury photographed alongside the villiage petrol pump in Tilford around 1925
(reproduced by kind permission of Mrs Winifred Harper-Smith, Mrs Amy Hall and Mrs Susan Allison)

William Tilbury and his wife Elizabeth were proprietors of the post Office and Shop in Tilford from its very beggining in the 1850's. Following Elizabeth's death in 1902, the property passed to her children Willie and Annie. A garage facility was added and this, together with the Post Office and Shop, were sold to John and Phyllis Wicks in 1946. The Business is now run by their daughter (Susan) and son-in-law (Brian Allison). Willie Tilbury's two daughters still live locally, Winifred Harper-Smith at Oak Cottage and Amy Hall at the Sands.

Although the 'horseless carriage' had been invented as early as the eighteenth century, it wasn't until the end of the nineteenth that a recognisable 'motor car' appeared on the roads. By then the roads had improved, thanks partly to the demands of cyclists who could not use their machines on the rutted tracks. In 1895, John Henry Knight of Farnham produced what was one of the first British cars to run on public roads. The car was a two-seater, three-wheeler, capable of reaching speeds of eight to twelve miles per hour. In 1903, Farnham Surveyor, Mr. Cass, had been instrumental in pioneering the use of tarred flints on road surfaces and by 1910, most of the main roads had a 'tarmacadam' surface. Tilford became more and more accessible to commuters and the influx of visitors increased; the first recorded car accident in Tilford occurred in January 1907 when one of the boys from All Saints school was knocked down by a motor car. Tilford and its surrounds was a popular area for military manoeuvres and

57. Troops at Tilford on way from Aldershot to Hankley Common c.1910
(reproduced by kind permission of the Old Kiln Museum Trust, Tilford)

Troop manoeuvres at Tilford and Hankley Common in the summer months were a common feature at the end of the 19th century and the beginning of the 20th. 'Grand Reviews' and 'sham fights' took place on Tilford Green and the school children were given half-day holidays to watch.

the arrival in the village of soldiers from Aldershot proved a great distraction for the children. Time and time again, the school log book reports that attendance is small 'owing to soldiers being in the village'. Often the pressure was so great that the school had to be closed. 'Sham fights', as they were called, between the soldiers attracted the most interest. The 'Empire' was regarded with almost religious fervour and in May, on Empire Day, there was much ceremonial. On May 27th 1908, the school logbook reports that the morning was a half-holiday and in the afternoon "Captain Moody RN [from Whitmead] gave out flags and gave an Empire address. The school then formed up in the playground and saluted the flag (hoisted by Jack Caesar, senior boy). This was followed by a prayer by the vicar and the national anthem." Tea and a prize distribution completed the service. In May of the following year, the Prince and Princess of Wales visited Tilford 'which was the centre of a large military operation' and of course, to mark this, the children were given yet another half-day holiday.

Ever since All Saints school opened, numbers had been steadily increasing. By the turn of the century the number of children on the books reached 80, double the number it had been thirty years earlier. A comprehensive report on the school made in 1904 was particularly damning. It noted that of the two departments, one for infants and the other for older pupils, the latter was full up and the former was in unsuitable accommodation. The report identified a number of faults such as the water supply which was 'by means of a well with a pump on the top of it situated in the playground'. The pump had been frozen on several occasions and the water had to be carried by hand for school and other purposes. Altogether, the report, covering eight pages, spoke of numerous things that were defective and concluded with a page of 'urgent structural alterations, additions or improvements necessary to bring the school up to a proper standard of efficiency.' It was estimated that £413.17s.6d. was needed to effect the changes required. Worse was to come. In 1905, the Sanitary Inspector having been alerted to several cases of sore throats and diphtheria, visited the school and condemned the sanitary arrangements as most unsatisfactory. All this had to be immediately put right.

Around the village, the building of 'grand' country houses in land released by the enclosures continued. Colonel John Davis, who had acquired the Whitmead Estate in 1886, erected a new house in 1894 to replace the old farmhouse on the site. With 17 bedrooms, it was an imposing building (but destined to be replaced by yet another grand house by the Berington family after the Second World War). Others, such as Charles Hill Court (Miss Lily Antrobus), Uplands (George Beaumont), Overwey (Lucy Margaret Lonsdale), followed shortly afterwards. Above Whitmead, John Hurd-Wood MD built a house that was to become the Whitmead Sanatorium for Consumptives; and in 1914, Henry Floyd built Highmead further up the hill. Tancred's Ford, along the Street and designed by Falkner, was built in 1913 for Mrs Watson who moved in in 1915. The First World War halted any further development and it was not until the 1920's that new houses began again to be built in the village.

Farming, which had seriously declined at the end of the nineteenth century, revived after the turn of the century and in 1914, produce was rising in value, the demand for farms was on the increase, rents were rising, higher wages were being paid, and generally farms were being better farmed. Before the war, hops were still a main crop in the village and as late as

1910, children were being given an extra weeks holiday in the summer 'on account of the hopping not being finished'. The need for more 'home-grown' food stimulated farming in Tilford whilst the demands for timber led to widespread tree felling. Trees were urgently required for war purposes and the felling around Black Lake and Crooksbury led to drastic changes in the landscape. After a Canadian Forestry Unit had been at work towards the end of the war, the view of Crooksbury was completely changed. "The trees" deplored George Sturt in his book *The Wheelwright's Shop* "cut into lengths, stripped of their bark and stacked in piles, gave to many an erst secluded hillside a staring publicity. This or that quiet place, the home of peace, was turned into a ghastly battle-field, with the naked and maimed corpses of tree lying about." Crooksbury, which up to then had been covered with trees, was reduced to 'a row of lonely pines' on the crest which stood out in the landscape for many miles.

At the outbreak of the war in 1914, there was probably a surfeit of labour in Tilford but with so many men required to serve in the armed forces, there was soon a shortage that was met by increased use of machinery and the employment of women on the land. Within a month of the appeal by Lord Kitchener for volunteers, 328 men between the ages of 18 and 30 had registered in the Corn Exchange in Farnham. Many of these were not to return. Tilford's War Memorial lists the names of 29 members of the village who gave up their lives in the service of their country between 1914 and 1918. These men came from families in the village, including the Lower Bourne, whose total numbers were around 700. The loss of over 4% of its population (or one eighth of its male workers) during the war was more than three times the national average and was a heavy sacrifice paid by the village.

Those left behind, too, played their part. At the start of the war, Waverley Abbey House, the home of Major and Mrs Rupert Anderson, was offered to the War Office as a Military Hospital for Other Ranks. It opened on the 18th September 1914 as an annexe to the Cambridge Hospital, Aldershot with Mrs Anderson as its Commandant. It had an operations theatre and 135 beds, and by the end of the war, 5,019 patients, mostly Belgian soldiers, had been cared for. Both Major Anderson, for his work in home defence and subsequently in the Royal Air Force, and Mrs Anderson, for her hospital work, were honoured by the award of the Order of the British

Empire after the war ended. Others, such as Mrs Caldwell Crofton of Heathyfield (now Sheephatch House) who was President of the Economy Campaign Committee in Farnham and who was active in promoting means of cooking on meagre rations, also worked at the hospital, as did Edith Ware, Martin Ware's sister.

58. Waverley Abbey Drawing Room used as a Hospital Ward during World War I
(reproduced by kind permission of the Old Kiln Museum Trust, Tilford)

On the outbreak of war in 1914, the owner of Waverly Abbey, Major Rupert D Anderson, offered the house to the War Office. It was opened on the 18th September 1914 as a military hospital under Mrs Rupert Anderson as Commandant, and remained open until April 1918.

Frensham Common provided the marshalling ground and training depot for Canadian troops before they were sent overseas. Trains brought them to Farnham where they assembled before marching on to Frensham. Military reviews were held on Hankley Common and distinguished leaders, such as Lloyd George and the Canadian Minister of Defence took the parade. On 18th July 1916, Dominion Day, a review of the 4th Canadian division was to be taken by King George V. Accompanied by Queen Mary, the King travelled by car from Aldershot to Tilford, calling in at Waverley *en route* to visit the hospital. Unlike a previous transit through Farnham in August 1915, when he was held up at the level crossing for several minutes, this journey went without incident. Coming over the West Bridge at Tilford, the King left his car in order to ride on horseback to Hankley. Writing in Tilford parish magazine in December 1992, Judith Ross gives this eyewitness story: "I was at Tilford school at the time and can remember how excited we all were at the thought of actually seeing the King. In the middle of the morning we walked two by two across the green to the big oak. A number of villagers had gathered there and an officer holding two horses stood by the tree. We did not have to wait long before a large black car crossed the bridge and stopped at the oak. The door opened and the King, in khaki uniform, stepped out. He and the officer saluted each other and seemed to talk for a minute or two, then the King mounted one horse, the officer the other, and they rode slowly, side by side, along the top of the green, past the school and up the hill."

For the children at the school, the war was a dreary time with shortages of food and the curtailment of amusements, and visits, such as that by the King, and the nearby presence of the military provided the few distractions open to them. In May 1916, the general gloom was partially lifted with the revival of the old Farnham fair. An idea of local farmers, it was opened by Rupert Anderson and raised over £1,600 for Red Cross funds. Later on that year, the school lost its headmaster, Mr. E. T. Philips, who 'having attested under Lord Derby's scheme and having been notified to report myself for service' left the school on the 13th of June. Occasionally, the children had their 'treats' such as entertainment in the Institute and 'games in the meadow adjoining Tilford House', but little else is recorded. They were clearly glad to see the end of the war, and on November 12th 1918, as the school logbook records, "the children assembled at the usual time when the Chairman of the Managers declared a day's holiday to celebrate the end of the Great War. Prayers and a hymn of thanksgiving were offered and lusty cheers were raised."

59. Tilford's War Memorial

Erected in 1919, Tilford's War Memorial has the names of the 29 men of Tilford who gave their lives in the Great War of 1914-1918 inscribed on its base. Behind it, is a stone tablet giving the names of the 23 parishoners who died on active service in the Second World War.

After the war ended and the village counted the extent of its loss, it was decided to erect a memorial to those in Tilford who had died as a result of enemy action during the war. A design based on a crucifix in Winchester Cathedral was chosen, subscriptions to meet the £460 needed were soon collected, and a site in All Saints churchyard was approved. The War Memorial was dedicated by the Bishop of Winchester on Sunday 2nd of November 1919. The inscription reads: "To the Glory of God and in grateful memory of the men of Tilford who gave their lives in the Great War 1914-1919."

By the 1920's, interest in development of land in Tilford returned and the Reverend Martin. S. Mare, who had inherited the Tilford House Estate from his uncle James Ware in 1902, released the remainder of the land he held as part of Woodhill Farm north of Whitmead Lane. The eastern part of the farm had been bought by Miss Lucy Lonsdale of Groombridge in Sussex in 1906 and 1907, for which she paid £2,108. On the 14 acres of land, she built Overwey and moved in in 1908; in 1910 she further extended the property by another 3 acres. In her negotiations with Martin Ware she was very concerned over what he would be doing with the remainder of the farmlands. In a letter to Ware, his solicitor remarks: "Miss Lonsdale was in fact apprehensive of your building cottages and villas, fearing that the motor omnibus which she thinks is to run from Haslemere to Farnham through Tilford will attract people to the villas." With the war intervening, it was not until 1926 that Ware was induced to sell the western half of the farm. Three large plots were reserved for larger houses (Archers Hill, Lane House and Tile House), the remainder of the land adjacent to the Street was taken up by those requiring smaller plots. By 1930, all the land had been sold and Woodhill Farm had ceased to be.

Meanwhile, the land along the Tilford to Hindhead road was being sold off. At the turn of the century there were only seven Tilford properties of any consequence strung out along the road south of the church - Stockbridge Cottages, Abbots Pond Cottage, The Duke of Cambridge Beer House, Abbots Villa (Whitefriars), Greenhills Lodge, Abbots Lodge, and South Bank Cottage (Gorse Cottage). There was plenty of room between them for development and this aspect was widely advertised. In 1903, H.G. Bunning, a builder from Godalming, purchased the allotment just south of Abbots Pond to build Abbots Cottage but apart from this, little happened before the First World War. The period afterwards, however, was one of determined house building. Farnham Rural District Council was the first to make a move; in January 1919, half an acre of land on the west side of the road (where Quest now stands) was purchased from Martin Ware for a council house estate. It is not clear why this didn't proceed - perhaps the cost of providing services was considered too great - whatever the case, the land was sold back to Ware in 1922 and a year later Colonel Bailey bought it (together with another half acre) for £100 on which he built Quest. Other prospective buyers saw their opportunity, and by 1932 nearly all the plots had been sold and houses had been built by their new owners.

The growth of Tilford in the north and to the south along the Hindhead road brought an increase in population of 25% in the early part of the 20th century, from just over 400 in 1891 to over 500 in 1921. The newcomers brought wealth into the village and this increased affluence demanded better services and improved facilities. Mains water had been supplied to houses in Farnham since 1836 but it wasn't until the turn of the century that this was extended outside the urban area with the establishment of the Wey Valley Water Company in Hindhead. Tilford was fortunate in having easy access to aquifers beneath the village and a good supply of water could be obtained from numerous individual wells. In the 19th century the larger houses had pumps to circulate the water to its destinations in the buildings. With more expensive houses being built there was a demand for mains

60. Drawing of Canon Martin Stewart Ware (1871-1934)
(reproduced by kind permission of Surrey History Service SHC 1576/44/10/2)

The Reverend Martin Stewart Ware was the nephew of James T. Ware and inherited Tilford House when his uncle died in 1902. After graduating from Cambridge, he was ordained priest in the Church of England in 1896 and was created Honorary Canon of Winchester in 1927.

water and this reached the village from boreholes sunk in Rushmoor (Wellesley Road). Later on, in 1932 and 1935, the Wey Valley Water Company would buy from Thomas Stovold the site in the Street (Tilford Meads) in which three boreholes now supplement the supply from Wellesley Road and Britty Hill in Elstead.

Electricity was first switched on in Farnham in May 1912 but it was not until 1927 that the Electric Lighting Order was extended to cover the rural areas around the town. Before that, lighting was by candles, acetylene, paraffin or petrol-gas lamps - although some of the big houses in Tilford had their own dynamos run by petrol engines. The choice facing those considering changing to electric light is well illustrated by a report considered by the Tilford Institute Management Committee on 4th March 1927. This noted that the installation would cost about £35.

The report came to the conclusion that: "the cost of upkeep would probably be not much less than the cost of the present system. Moreover, that although there are certain advantages in electric light, such as cleanliness, convenience, labour saving and in certain directions safety" the facts were "that the Institute is used in the evening when light is needed by comparatively few members on most occasions and that the dances are attended by people who live outside Tilford." The report ended by asking "whether it would be fair to call on Tilford residents to raise a capital sum by subscription to meet the initial cost of installing light in the Institute." The meeting decided against. A year and a half later, however, they changed their minds and opened the 'Tilford Institute Electric Light Account'.

Houses slowly connected to the system although the cost of connecting to the mains deterred many from having electricity in the home even though the mains ran along the road outside. All Saints School didn't install electric lighting until September 1945, and as late as 1951, properties in Reeds Road had no mains electricity supply. At the same time as laying on electricity, the Farnham Gas and Electricity Company brought mains gas into Tilford. Householders connected to this more readily than they did to the electric mains - possibly because whilst gas could be used for both heating and lighting, electricity was restricted to the latter.

61. The Hunt sets off from Tilford Green c.1950
(reproduced by kind permission of Mrs Estelle Carter, Sheephatch Farm, Tilford)

Hunting, Shooting, and Fishing have been traditional pursuits in Tilford over the centuries. Horse-riding continues to grow in popularity and many equestrian facilities are on offer in the village.

With increased affluence came also increased opportunities for recreation. Hunting, shooting and fishing had been the traditional country sports practised by the gentry and these continued to be enjoyed by the newcomers. In addition, horse riding, cycling and walking became popular in the area and local sports activities and clubs were strongly supported. The Institute, situated as it was on the village green, provided a focus and a venue for many of these activities some of which, such as cricket on the green and the Tilford Fife and Drum Band, predated it. Tilford cricket has for a long time been synonymous with sport in the village and its story is well told in Graham Collyer's book *Tilford Cricket Club*, published in 1985 to mark its centenary.

Another popular sport, but one that has fallen into disuse, was football. Tilford Football Club was flourishing before 1920 when it was affiliated into the Institute under the same conditions as the cricket club. Tilford football attracted a strong following in between the wars, the club winning the Farnham Football League Division II Cup in 1926. In abeyance during the Second World War, football was revived in 1946 and received a boost in 1949 when Mr Price of Shortheath Lodge in Farnham, gave the village six acres of land at Stonehills for a recreation ground. The land, however, was never developed and interest in Tilford football faded. An attempt to resuscitate it was made in 1959 but didn't get off the ground, and in 1968, the Institute removed it from the list of affiliated clubs. Other sports have included tennis (a Tilford Institute Tennis Club was formed in 1923 and continued until 1940), billiards, and snooker. A bowling green at the Institute was formally opened in 1926 but only lasted five years. A Tilford Artisans Golf Club was active from 1920 to 1950.

62. Tilford Horticultural Society Commitee 1930's
(reproduced by kind permission of the Thomas Family Archives)

In the early days, members of the Tilford Horticultural Society fell into two classes: 'Ordinary' and 'Honorary'. The ordinary members were these actively involved in the gardening profession. The 1930's committtee was composed exclusively of ordinary members, eight of whom were gardeners or head gardeners in the big Tilford properties.

Of the other village societies and clubs, the Tilford Horticultural Society is the oldest still in existence with records going back to 1905. In the early days, there were two distinct classes of members: honorary and ordinary. The so-called ordinary members were the professional gardeners employed in the various big houses; the honorary members were the gentry. Ordinary members paid one or two shillings a year subscription whilst honorary members paid in guineas. There was an annual flower show at which the band would perform and amusements and dancing would be an extra diversion. This replaced the annual fair which had been held on Tilford Green from time immemorial and which later developed into the Tilford Fete. Tilford Institute has spawned many specialist groups such as the Men's Club, the Women's Club - both active in the 1920's, a Boy's Club and a Girl's Club in the 1930's and 40's, a Youth Club started in the 50's, and currently the Tilford Toddlers and the Youth Drop-in Centre. In October 1921, the idea of forming a Tilford Dramatic Club at the Institute was mooted. This later developed into the 'Tilford Players' who gave their first performance under that name in 1934. Disbanded during the Second World War, they were revived in 1947 in association with a newly-formed Arts Group at the Institute, and apart from one or two breaks in the 1950's and 70's, have given a full programme of theatrical performances ever since.

Behind many of the social activities in the village has been the Tilford Women's Institute which was formed on the 17th February 1924 and grew out of weekly meetings held by Mrs Margaret Ware at Tilford House. It has remained continuously active throughout its life and remains a flourishing organisation today. There was a Tilford Brass Band in the 1920's, a Nurses Association formed just after WWII, an Animal Protection Society formed in 1967, and a very successful 'Over 60's Club' which functioned from 1960 until 1984. One organisation that has achieved national and international recognition is the Tilford Bach Society which was formed in 1952 by Denys Darlow the organist at Tilford Church. Starting from modest beginnings it has grown into a highly acclaimed professional organisation which has become famous for the Tilford Bach Festival which it promotes every year.

It was in the 1930's that the strength of the 'Tilford lobby' began to be seen. Under the Local Government Act of 1894, powers had been transferred from the Farnham Vestry to Farnham Rural District Council that initially comprised Hale, Wrecclesham and Tilford. In 1914, Hale was absorbed into Farnham Urban District and in 1924, Wrecclesham went the same way, leaving Tilford as the sole remaining member of the Rural District. The imminent changes to be made under the Surrey Review Order of 1933, under which it was proposed that Tilford should also be incorporated into Farnham Urban District Council, was opposed by the Ministry of Health on the grounds that none of Tilford's services (water, gas, electricity, or sewerage) were provided by Farnham. The residents of Tilford were wholly behind the Ministry and against Surrey County Council. At an emergency meeting of Tilford parishioners, held in a packed Institute in June 1932, it was unanimously agreed that the village sided with the Minister of Health and that the residents did not want to be 'urbanised'. When the Surrey Review Order was published on 31st January 1933, it declared that, as from 1st April, Tilford would be a separate civil parish coming under the newly-formed Hambledon Rural District Council (absorbed into Waverley District Council in 1974). Its boundaries were re-defined (leaving out Lower Bourne which became part of Farnham) and five councillors (raised to seven in 1937) were nominated to form a newly-christened Tilford Parish Council. From then on the village has managed its own local affairs and has been independent of the town of Farnham to which it had previously been attached ever since records began.

Except for Woodhill, which had been established farmland, the only land sold to developers up to the mid 1930's was from the enclosed waste. This was to change. In 1937, Thomas Stovold died and his estate was put up for auction. Unlike the last estate auction sale - that of Waverley Abbey in 1870 - which was sold as a single unit, this one was offered piecemeal in eighteen lots. The majority of the estate was purchased by Miss Caroline Mary Hazell of Farnham for £6,550. She quickly disposed of many of the lots along the Street with Street Farm going to Mr and Mrs Skelton and Upper Street Farm going to William North. The land behind the Post Office was sold to the occupying tenants Willie and Annie Tilbury, whilst Frank Alderton, the builder, bought the land leading to what was to become Riversmeet, and Mr Gibby, another builder, plots on the south side of Squires Hill Lane.

With land becoming available, consideration was given to founding a secondary school in the village and a group of 'promoters' was formed to raise funds and purchase a suitable building plot. The area chosen was the land to the south of Squires Hill Lane to the west of what was to become Shepherds Way, and in 1939 Canon George Buchanan, on behalf of the promoters, purchased this site from Caroline Hazell. The plans had been approved by the Ministry of Education and it was hoped to have the school in place by September 1940. However, the war put a stop to all such plans and it was not until 1946 that the matter could be reopened. By then, the 1944 Education Act had laid down that secondary schools required a minimum area of 11 acres and as the site purchased in 1939 was only 7 acres, the location was changed to the present site of Waverley Abbey School which was acquired by compulsory purchase in 1949. The school finally opened in 1952.

63. Home Guard No 3 (Crooksbury and Tilford) Platoon, 1944
(reproduced by kind permission of the Old Kiln Museum Trust)

Known affectionately as 'Dad's Army' the Home Guard was formed during the Second World War to supplement and support the regular forces in the local area.

The Second World War put an end to most building initiatives in Tilford and all efforts were directed at meeting the challenges imposed by wartime conditions and coping with the difficulties they brought. Air Raid Precautions (ARP) were rehearsed during the so-called 'appeasement' period of 1938 and a 'Tilford and Crooksbury Platoon' of the Home Guard was formed. Early in 1939 a Wardens' Service was established with the village divided into four sectors, North, Central, Middle West and West. Amongst their many duties in seeing that wartime procedures were being carried out, the wardens were responsible for assembling, issuing, and fitting gas masks and securing and storing emergency food rations in various houses in the village. Tilford established a reputation for its ARP services and was recognised as the most efficient in the Guildford area. Women's organisations were heavily involved and the local Red Cross, based on the Institute, was ready for first-aid, nursing, and gas decontamination. The Women's Voluntary Service was also very active in caring for those in need in the village.

All round the village, 'pillboxes' and anti-tank obstacles were erected, and in the woods behind the Rural Life Centre dugouts for the use of Auxiliary Units to be deployed behind enemy lines should they pass through Tilford, were constructed. Altogether some 36 sites in Tilford, where Second World War military defences are to be found, have been identified. On Hankley

Common, a wall was built by the Canadian Army Engineers to simulate what the invading troops could expect to meet when they landed in France on 'D-day'. Exercises by troops and tanks rehearsing their assaults on the wall are said to have shaken Tilford with the violence of the noise. The village had its share of enemy bombs: screamers, high explosive, incendiaries, phosphorous, armour-piercing, parachute-mines, and the 'doodle-bug' rocket. Many bombs landed on Hankley Common, 11 bombs are known to have fallen near Tilford Mill, a 'doodle-bug' landed at the back of Birchen Reeds, and land mines are reported to have fallen at the rear of the church. In 1952, two anti-tank mines were found when the 'island' close to the East Bridge was cleared, and mines were still being unearthed by forestry workers in Tilford as late as 1969. Although there were many occasions, particularly during 1940, when life in Tilford was disrupted by the warning sound of the air raid sirens, it was at night that the bombs fell on the village when, as All Saints school log reports, 'children were very tired' having had 'disturbed nights all week'.

At Sheephatch, following the 'Camp Act' of 1939, a camp school was established to accommodate evacuees and in April 1940, evacuees from Leyton in Essex and Walthamstow in London came to Tilford where they stayed until they reached school-leaving age. Sheephatch School closed temporarily in April 1943 but reopened three years later in February 1946 as a co-educational boarding school. Other children evacuated from London lived with friends in the village swelling the numbers attending All Saints school. Canadian soldiers were very much in evidence and were billeted in some of Tilford's houses. In 1941, army engineers built a bridge across the Wey to supplement Tilford's mediaeval West Bridge and this 'temporary' wartime bridge remains in use to this day.

At the end of the war, Tilford once again had the sad duty of counting its dead. A stone tablet was erected on the wall behind the War Memorial on which the names of the twenty-three parishioners who had died on active duty in the war were inscribed.

Immediately after the war, like their predecessors Farnham Rural District Council had attempted in 1919, Hambledon Rural District Council sought to build low cost houses in Tilford. The site chosen was between the Riversmeet houses and Squires Hill Lane. In 1946 the Council acquired a parcel of land from Miss Hazell's executors west of Devona, sufficient to build four houses; a new road was constructed and the name of 'Squires Way' was suggested. In deference to the long-standing name of the site, however, it was decided to call it 'Shepherd's Way'. Hambledon was persuaded of the need to expand the Shepherd's Way estate and a year later, it acquired a further two plots for another fifteen houses; but except for two additional bungalows, was unable to proceed further because of the lack of mains drainage. A small sewage disposal works had been built as part of the Shepherd's Way construction programme but this could not accommodate any more load. It wasn't until 1997 that Hambledon's successors, Waverley District Council, were in a position to admit more tenants to the site.

Mains drainage had been a problem for the village for many years. Farnham had installed its first main sewer in 1888 and the Rural District Council extended it along the Tilford Road in 1899. Tilford, however, was too far from Farnham to justify the cost of connection and it had to wait until Hambledon Rural District was formed in 1933 before any constructive advances could be made. In 1936 a proposed scheme was put up for consideration but met with objections from Tilford Parish Council and was dropped. The concern of the Council was the location of the sewage disposal works which, it had been proposed, should be at Whitmead. The matter was left in abeyance during the war, to be resurrected in 1951 when Hambledon set out a scheme that included sewage disposal works on Hankley Common. Tilford Parish Council was reasonably happy with this proposal but it wasn't until 1969 that Hambledon produced a comprehensive sewerage scheme for the western section of the district that would bring Tilford on line. Difficulties over the site for a pumping station in the village continued to be an obstacle to progress and it was a year later before final agreement was reached for this to be near the west bridge alongside Malthouse Farm.

Work began in April 1971 and accompanied by continuing objections to the routing of some of the pipes, was finished by the end of the year. The cost of connection was high and many households continued to use the septic tanks that had served them well in the past. Alongside the protracted discussions on main sewerage had been a similar debate on the provision of a public lavatory in the village. With so many visitors to Tilford the need for such a facility became more and more urgent, but the lack of sewerage facilities and heated arguments over its location delayed its construction until 1983.

The break-up of the Stovold Estate was followed by the dismantling of the other major Tilford landholdings. During the war, in 1940, the vast Pierrepont Estate of 2,655 acres was put up for sale. The estate extended eastwards covering the south-west of Tilford including Tankersford Common and Tilford Common. Around the turn of the century, two cottages (Well and Eliot) had been built but other than this, no development had taken place in this part of Tilford. In 1946, Mrs Anderson put the Waverley Abbey Estate of 768 acres up for sale and moved back to Squires Hill House which her husband, Major Rupert Darnley Anderson, had built in 1898. The major part of the estate, including the mansion and the Waverley Abbey ruins, were bought by Mr A J Whitehead. The remainder including Sheephatch Farm, Heathyfield (Sheephatch House), Waverley Mill and most of the cottages in Crooksbury, were sold to individuals.

Four years later, in 1950, Whitehead put the estate, now consisting of 485 acres under the auctioneer's hammer. Headlined in the Farnham Herald as 'Historic Estate Broken Up', it was the final chapter in the story of Tilford's big landholdings. "One by one" said the Herald "the large country estates of England are being split up, and it was no surprise when the auctioneers failed to sell the Waverley Abbey Estate as a whole when it was offered [for auction]." The mansion itself was bought by Mrs Mayo-Perrott and became, first, a residential hotel and later, in 1983, a Christian Conference Centre run by the Crusade for World Revival.

The grounds on which stand the ruins of the once great Abbey were acquired by the North family before being taken over by the Department of Environment in 1973. The year before, Tilford House Estate (now reduced to 630 acres) had been auctioned. Described in the catalogue as 'two useful dairy farms, an old world cottage residence, and fifteen cottages together with agricultural land, heath and woodland', it marked the end of the hegemony built up by the Ware family over more than a hundred years.

The present-day pattern of houses in Tilford was by now almost complete. On Crooksbury Hill, the cottages such as Cobbett's Corner, Crooksbury

Cottage, Keeper's Cottage, Mount Pleasant Farm, Waverley Cottage, Waverley Hollow and Yew Tree Cottage, were of long-standing; the remainder have been built in the twentieth century. The once-ubiquitous heathlands comprising the Tilford waste have now nearly all been converted to plantations, now mostly in private hands. A small area in the south-west of Tilford is part of the National Trust's Frensham Pond's complex; the land at the summit of Crooksbury Hill is owned by Surrey County Council; and the land at the back of the Church was bought by Hambledon RDC from the Cottingham Timber Company in 1952 and houses a camping site.

As we have seen in a previous chapter, the use of Tilford's waste land for forestry dates back to the eighteenth century when Sir Robert Rich of Waverley Abbey planted 12 acres of Crooksbury Hill with fir trees. Following the success of this initiative, in 1794 the Board of Agriculture made a general recommendation that heathlands should be profitably used by planting with Scots fir or larch. In consequence, heathlands have been markedly reduced over the whole of Surrey, completely altering the landscape in areas such as Tilford. In Tilford, forestry and its associated nursery facilities is now a major industry and it has been recorded that the village produces more trees than any other comparable village in the UK.

A leading entrepreneur in this field was Archibald (Archie) Aitkins who purchased Tilhill House and its 20 acres of land in 1947 to create Tilford's first tree nursery. The nursery filled a much-needed gap in the market and flourished so well that in 1953 Archie leased 120 acres of Tankersford Common to support his expanding business. In 1958, he acquired 140 acres of land at Greenhills and transferred both his business and the name of Tilhill there. Tilhill Forestry has employed many local people among whom was Henry Jackson its former Managing Director. In 1969 Henry and his wife Madge started collecting agricultural artefacts at their home, 'The Old Kiln', along the Reeds road. The collection together with an arboretum has grown to fill ten acres and was opened to the public as a museum, 'The Rural Life Centre', in April 1973.

A major development in the village occurred in 1984 when the 27-acre site of Sheephatch School was bought by Surrey County Council. As noted earlier, this co-educational boarding school, which closed in 1977 after 31 years in operation, was the successor of the 'Camp' school which had accommodated evacuees during the war and had been left derelict awaiting a purchaser. It was bought by the Ahmadiyya Muslim Association UK who renamed it the 'Ahmadiyya Muslim Centre-Islamabad' and who use it to cater for the religious, cultural and social needs of its members. Although the resident community is small, the week-end residential schools and rallies bring many visitors to the village and a major impact is felt over the last week of each July when over 20,000 participants are attracted to the Association's three-day convention at the Centre.

64. Ahmadiyya Convention at Isamabad, Tilford
(reproduced by kind permission of the Ahmadiyya Muslim Association UK)

Islamabad in Tilford is the Home of the UK's Ahmadiyya Muslim Association. Its annual conventions attract over twenty thousand followers from the UK and over.seas

Today, Tilford is a much sought-after village with a village green bounded by the river Wey and two picturesque mediaeval bridges. Its 700 inhabitants are served by three public houses and a village post office, shop and garage; seven plant nurseries offer their wares. Flanking the green are the Church, the Infant School, and the Institute whilst further up the Street is the Junior School. Both schools cater for children from a wide area around Tilford. The central area of the village contains many houses of

65. The Barley Mow and Cricket on Tilford Green

Cricket on the Green is the scene many identify with Tilford and the village has used as the setting for a number of cricket events broadcast on radio and television.

historical interest and was classified as a Conservation Area in 1973. A Parish Council, comprising seven elected members, serves the community which also elects representatives for Waverley Borough Council and Surrey County Council. The Institute continues to be the focus for the village's social and sports activities of which cricket remains the most prominent. In addition to the long-standing village associations such as the Tilford Horticultural Society, the Tilford Players, the Tilford Bach Society, and the Women's Institute, there are new organisations such as the Tilford Toddlers and the Tilford Meadows Nursery School. There is limited fishing in Stockbridge Pond and in the river, and Hankley Common Golf Club and the Frensham Riding Club offer local sporting facilities. There are plentiful opportunities for horse riding and for walking along the many attractive bridle paths around the village and a site alongside the Hankley Public House offers caravan accommodation. Although Waverley Abbey lies outside the Civil Parish of Tilford, it comes within the Ecclesiastical Parish and is often considered to be part of Tilford. The ruins afford a strong link with the past and a powerful reminder of Tilford's long and absorbing history.

This won't be the end of the story of Tilford. In the years to come, many new developments will take place and future historians will, with the advantages of hindsight, see in the happenings of today the seeds of impending change. This is not within our lot to forecast. But the attractions of Tilford which have served it so well in the past will undoubtedly continue to do so in the future, drawing people to live and work in the village with the same sense of pride and belonging that has been Tilford's enduring character down the centuries.

Glossary

Acre	A measure of area equal to 4,840 square yards or about 4,050 square metres (0.4050 hectares).
Barrow	A mound of earth or stones covering one or more burials.
Bondland	Land that was owned by the Lord of the Manor and let out to tenants and to which boonwork *(q.v.)* was attached.
Bondman	A tenant of the manor who was 'bound' to the Lord of the Manor and could not leave without his permission.
Boonwork	A duty owed to the Lord of the Manor to work on his demesne *(q.v.)* additional to customary labour service.
Bordar	A villein cottager.
Copyhold	A form of tenure by which the tenant held a copy of the entry in the manorial court rolls. The tenancy could be sold by the 'copyholder' or passed on to his heirs; in every case a *fine (q.v.)* had to be paid to the Lord of the Manor.
Cottar	A cottager.
Croft	An enclosed meadow or arable land usually adjacent to a house
Demesne	Land on the manor that was reserved for the Lord of the Manor's own use.
Domus	A home.
Estover	The right to take wood from common land for fuel or repair of houses.
Farthing	A quarter of a virgate *(q.v.) i.e.* an area of about $7^{1}/_{2}$ acres.
Fine	A payment made to the Lord of the Manor whenever there was a transfer of title of land.

Hatch	A fenced area of land. The 'hatch' came to mean 'gateway'. In Tilford the word is used in connection with 'Sheephatch'.
Heriot	An obligation on an heir to provide the best live beast or chattel of a deceased tenant to the Lord of the Manor. It was later replaced by a monetary payment and was abolished in 1922.
Hide	The amount of land that could be ploughed in a year using one plough with an eight-ox team. The measurement varied with the quality of the soil. In Surrey it generally comprised 120 acres.
Hundred	Originally an area of 100 families which later became a useful administrative division.
Lay Subsidy	A tax paid to the crown by lay people (as opposed to clerics). Originally it was a ten percent tax on people's moveable items; later it became a tax on land and goods, one tenth for town residents and one fifteenth for country dwellers.
Manor	A territory held in feudal tenure by the Lord of the Manor. Tilford was part of Farnham Manor whose Lord was the Bishop of Winchester.
Mead	A meadow. In Tilford, present-day Whitmead was originally a so-called 'wide meadow'
Mesolithic	Middle Stone Age, starting at the end of the last ice age about 10,000 years ago and ending with the advent of the Neolithic Age.
Messuage	A dwelling house and its surrounding property.
Moor	Rough land often with a stream passing through it.
Neolithic	New Stone Age. Characterised by farming communities as opposed to the hunter-gatherers of the Mesolithic Age. Considerable difficulty surrounds the dating of the Mesolithic/Neolithic transition in southern Britain but a date of 4500 BC would appear to be not too far out.
Palaeolithic	Old Stone Age, dating from when hominids first appeared (some half a million years ago in Surrey) up to the start of the

	Mesolithic Age. The period when modern man (*homo sapiens sapiens*) appeared (around 40,000 years ago in Surrey) is referred to as the 'Upper Palaeolithic' Age.
Pannage	Payment made to the Lord of the Manor for the feeding of swine in a wood.
Perch	A measure of area one fortieth of a rood *(q.v.) i.e.* one 160th of an acre; or can be used as a measurement of length equal to 1 rod *(q.v.)*.
Purpresture	Land taken out of the waste *(q.v.)* and to which no boonwork *(q.v.)* was attached.
Rector	The person appointed to the benefice of a parish and who received the tithes of the parishioners. After the dissolution of the monasteries, the rector's rights were often purchased by lay people who kept a large part of the tithes (the 'great tithes') to themselves, appointing a vicar - who received a small part (the 'little tithes') - to serve in their place.
Reeds	Cleared land *e.g.* land from the waste cleared for grazing
Rod	A measure of length of $16^{1}/_{2}$ feet ($5^{1}/_{2}$ yards).
Rood	A measure of area one quarter of an acre (*i.e.* 40 square rods or perches).
Tithing	Originally a company of ten householders who stood security for each other within a system called Frankpledge. Later it became a land division, once regarded as a tenth of a hundred. Farnham Hundred comprised the tithings of Wreclesham (Wrecclesham), Ronewyk (Runwick), Fermesham (Frensham), Cherte or Charte (Churt), Ellestede (Elstead), Tylleford (Tilford), Ronevalle (Runfold), Thwongham (Tongham), Batshate (Badshot), and Comptone (Compton). Bourne and Rowledge were once part of Wrecclesham; Hale including Upper Hale and Weybourne replaced Badshot; the 'tithing' of Dogflud or Dogfleet is merged with the south-eastern part of Farnham town; and Seale and Tongham have replaced Tongham. Waverley was *ex parochial* and outside the hundred.

Tithingman	The elected representative of a tithing (*q.v.*) responsible for presenting the misdemeanours of his members to the court; the forerunner of the police constable.
Turbary	The right to dig peat or turves for fuel on the commons
Toft	A plot which was previously occupied by a messuage (*q.v.*) but now no longer.
Villein	An unfree tenant.
Virgate	Quarter of a Hide. A variable quantity of land area depending on the quality of the soil and amounting in Tilford to 30 acres.
Waste	Common land from which no rent or tax was forthcoming.
Yardland	Another name for a Virgate (*q.v.*); sometimes abbreviated to 'yard'.

Further Reading

General

'Historical Britain', E. S. Wood, (1995), Harvill.
'The History of the Countryside', O. Rackham, (1986), Weidenfeld & Nicholson.
'Trees and Woodland in the British Landscape', O. Rackham, (1976), Weidenfeld & Nicholson.
'The Parish Chest', W. E. Tate, (1946), Phillimore.
'The Oxford Companion to Local and Family History', D. Hey, (1996), OUP.
'The Local Historian's Encyclopaedia', J. Richardson, (1974), Historical Publications.
'The Making of the English Landscape', W. G. Hoskins, (1983), Penguin.
'Victoria County History, Surrey', (ed.) H. E. Malden, Vol. 1(1902) and Vol. 2 (1905), Constable.
'A History of Surrey', Henry E. Malden, (1905), Eliot Stock.
'The Surrey Landscape', G. Clark & W. Harding Thompson, (1934), Black.
'History of the Antiquities of Surrey', O. Manning and W. Bray, (1814).
'History of Surrey & Sussex', Thomas Allen, (1829).
'The Place of Surrey in the History of England', F. J. C. Hearnshaw, (1936), Macmillan.
'History of Farnham and the Ancient Cistercian Abbey at Waverley', W. C. Smith, (1829).
'Old Surrey Water Mills', J. Hillier, (1851), Skeffington.

Chapter One: Facts and Figures

'Surrey Local Names', Gerald S Davies, (1881).
'The Place Names of England and Wales', Rev. J.B.Johnston, (1914).
'English Place-Name Elements', A.H.Smith, (1956).
'Concise Oxford Dictionary of English Place-Names', (1960).
'The Place Names of Surrey', J.E.B.Gover, A.Mawer and F.M.Stenton, (1982), English Place Names Society.
'Pre-1841 Censuses & Population Listings in the British Isles', Colin R. Chapman, (1994), Lochin, 3rd edn.
'Domesday Book, 3 Surrey', ed. John Morris, (1975), Phillimore.

Chapter Two: Landscape and Land

'The Wealden District', Gallois, R.W., 4th edn, (1965). HMSO.
'A Survey of the Prehistory of the Farnham District', Oakley, K.P., Rankine, W.F.& Lowther, A.W.G., (1939), Surrey Archaeological Collections.
'The Historical Atlas of the Earth', R. Osborne and D. Tarling, (1996), Henry Holt.

Chapter Three: Prehistoric Tilford

'The Archaeology of Surrey to 1540', (ed.) Joanna Bird and D.G. Bird, (1987), Surrey Archaeological Society.
'The South East to AD 1000', Peter Drewett, David Rudling, & Mark Gardiner, (1988), Longman.

Chapter Four: The Roman Occupation

'The Archaeology of Surrey to 1540', (ed.) Joanna Bird and D.G. Bird, (1987), Surrey Archaeological Society.
'A History of Surrey', H.E. Malden, (1900), E.P.Publishing Ltd., facsimile edition, (1977).
'The South East to AD 1000', Peter Drewett, David Rudling, & Mark Gardiner, (1988), Longman.
'The Conquest of Gaul', Julius Caesar, (1953), Penguin.

Chapter Five: The Dark Ages

'The Archaeology of Surrey to 1540', (ed.) Joanna Bird and D.G. Bird, (1987), Surrey Archaeological Society.
'Early Medieval Surrey', John Blair, (1991), Alan Sutton & Surrey Archaeological Society.
'Saxon Farnham', Elfrida Manning, Phillimore, (1970).
'The South East to AD 1000', Peter Drewett, David Rudling, & Mark Gardiner, (1988), Longman.
'The Anglo-Saxon Chronicles', (ed.) A. Savage, (1996), Coombe Books.

Chapter Six: The Coming of the Normans

'The South East from AD 1000', Peter Brandon & Brian Short, (1990), Longman.
'A Little History of the Abbey of S. Mary of Waverley', Etienne Robo, (1928), Langham.
'The White Monks of Waverley', Gwen Ware, (1976), Farnham & District Museum Society.
'Waverley Abbey', Harold Brakspear, (1905), Surrey Archaeological Society.
'A History of Waverley Abbey in the County of Surrey', C, Kerry, (1872), Andrews.

Chapter Seven: Mediaeval Tilford

'Early Mediaeval Surrey', John Blair, (1991), Sutton.
'The Black Death', P. Zeigler, (1988), Penguin.
'Mediaeval Farnham', Etienne Robo, (1935), Langham.
'Sir Nigel', Arthur Conan Doyle, (1906), Smith & Elder.

Chapter Eight: Tudor Times

'Sixteenth Century England', J. Youings, (1988), Penguin.
'Farnham and its Borough', Rev R. N. Milford, (1858), Longman.

Chapter Nine: The Civil War and its Aftermath

'Britannia: Surrey and Sussex', William Camden, 1607.
'Farnham During the Civil Wars and Interregnum', D. E. Hall & F. Gretton, Farnham Castle Newspapers.

Chapter Ten: The Landed Gentry

'The Natural History and Antiquities of the County of Surrey', John Aubrey, (1719).
'A Tour through England & Wales', Daniel Defoe, (1722).
'Frensham, Then and Now', Baker & Minchin, (1938), Langham.
'Mark Wilton, the Merchant's Clerk', Charles Tayler, (1848), Chapman & Hall.
'Western Tour', Gilpin, 1798.

Chapter Eleven: Paternalism and Change

'Reshaping Rural England', A. Howkins, (1991), Routledge.
'Victorian Farnham', Ewbank Smith, (1971), Phillimore.
'Farnham Inheritance', Nigel Temple, (1965), Langham.
'Reminiscences of a Country Town (Farnham)', John Henry Knight, (1909), Martin & Stuart.
'A Farnham Souvenir', W. Chapman, (1869), John Nicholls.
'Farnham and its Borough', Rev R. N. Milford, (1858), Longman.
'Tilford through the Ages', G. Collyer et. al., (1996).
'Tilford Cricket Club: 1885-1985', Graham Collyer, (1985), Simpson Drewett.
'Rural Rides', W. Cobbett, (1830), Penguin Books (1985).
'Change in the Village', George Bourne, (1912), Duckworth.
'Memoirs of a Surrey Labourer', George Bourne, (1907), Duckworth.
'A Small Boy in the Sixties', George Sturt, (1927), CUP.
'William Smith, Potter & Farmer', George Bourne, (1919), Chatto & Windus
'Journals of George Sturt', (ed.) G. Grigson, (1941), Cresset Press.
'We Two', Edna Lyall, (1898), Hurst & Blackett.
'Remembrances of Life & Customs in Gilbert White's, Cobbett's and Charles Kingsley's Country', J. A. Eggar, (1924), F. Sturt.
'Salt and his Circle', S. Winsten, Hutchinson.
'The English Gardener', William Cobbett, (1828), A. Cobbett.
'Old West Surrey', Gertrude Jekyll, (1904), Longmans.

Chapter Twelve: Progress and Plenty

'Edwardian Farnham', Ewbank Smith, (1979), Charles Hammick.
'Farnham in War and Peace', Ewbank Smith, (1983), Phillimore.
'Outside the Garden', Helen Milman, (1900), Lane.
'Picture a Country Vicarage', Anthony Brode, (1957), The Country Book Club.

Primary Source Material from:

All Saints Vicarage, Tilford Road, Tilford, Surrey GU10 2DA.
The British Library, 96 Euston Road, London NW1 2DB.
The British Library Newspaper Library, Colindale Avenue, London NW9 5HE.
Church of England Record Centre, 15 Galleywall Road, South Bermondsey, London SE16 3PB.
Family Records Centre, 1 Myddelton Street, London EC1R 1UW
Museum of Farnham, Willmer House, 38 West Street, Farnham, Surrey GU9 7DX.
Hampshire Record Office, Sussex Street, Winchester, Hampshire SO23 8TH.
Hyde Park Family History Centre, 64/68 Exhibition Road, London SW7 2PA.
Institute of Historical Research, University of London, Senate House, Malet Street, London WC1E 7HU.
London Metropolitan Archives, 40 Northampton Road, London EC1R 0HB.
The Minet Library, 52 Knatchbull Road, Lambeth, London SE5 9QY.
National Register of Archives, Quality House, Quality Court, Chancery Lane, London WC2A 1HP.
Office for National Statistics, 1 Drummond Gate, London SW1V 2QQ.
Probate Registry, First Avenue House, 42-49 High Holborn, London WC1V 6NP.
Public Record Office, Ruskin Avenue, Kew, Surrey TW9 4DU.
Rural History Centre, University of Reading, Whiteknights, Reading, Berkshire RG6 6AG.
Rural Life Centre, Old Kiln Museum, Reeds Road, Tilford, Surrey GU10 2DL.
Society of Genealogists, 14 Charterhouse Buildings, Goswell Road, London EC1M 7BA.
Surrey Archaeological Society, Castle Arch, Guildford, Surrey GU1 3SX.
Surrey History Centre, 139 Goldsworth Road, Woking, Surrey GU21 1ND.

Index

*Numbers in **bold** refer to the illustration captions.*

Abney, 72-3, 80, 82, 84, 113.
Agriculture & Forestry, 14, 39, 43, 44, 46, 49, 59, 60, 62, 66, 69-70, 93, 104, 117, 121, 132.
Ahmadiyya Muslim Association UK, 133.
Aislabie, William, 62.
Aitkins, Archie, 132.
Alderton, 127.
Alice Holt, 20, 21.
Anderson, 82, 96, 106, 114, 118, 131.
Antrobus, Lily, 117.
Archaeological Remains, 11, 15-7, **15**, **19**, 29, 22, 24
Bailey, Col., 122
Baker, John, 81.
Barnett, Elizabeth, 81.
Barrows, 14-6.
Barton, Edward, 59.
Beaumont, George, 117.
Beating the Bounds, 5.
Beldham, 81, **104**, 105, **112**.
Berington, 117.
Black Death, 7, 49-51, 54, 56, 58, 60, **61**, 62.
Bourne, 5, 6, 32, 37, 91, 107, 118, 127.
Boxfold, Harry, 54.
Bradbridge, Richard, 59.
Bronze Age, 14, 17.
Brooks, Philip, 42.
Browne, Sir Anthony, 53-4.
Buchanan, Canon 27, 28.
Burden, Dr Francis, **85**, 87.
Caedwalla, 25-6, **25**, 27 28, 35.
Caesar, 18, 94, 105, 116.
Caldwell, Crofton, 114, 119.
Canadians, 119, 129.
Caravans, 134.
Census, 6-7, 89
Chapman, Arthur, 96
Charters, 6, **29**, 26, **27**, 28, 33, 49.
Chitty, Robert,
Christian, 102, 108.

Churt, 1,5, 42, 46, 48, 68, 107.
Cobbett, 73, 77, 112.
Coldham, John, 54, 62, 76.
Combe, Richard, 107.
Compton, 5, 75, 77.
Conan Doyle, 39.
Cricket, 105, 107, 134, **134**.
Cromwell, Oliver, 64.
Crusade for World Revival, 131.
Danes, 30.
Davis, John, 64, 96, 105, 108, 117.
Davison, Crawford, 80, 83, 87, 98, 99, 107.
De Blois, Henry, 37, 39.
De Roemer, Major Martin, 20, **20**.
Dinosaurs, 8.
Dissenters, 85, **85**.
Dodds, Rev Henry, 86, 87.
Domesday Survey, 6-7, 32-33, 48
Eade, 103-4, **103**.
Eashing, 28.
Edge, the Rev, 12, **13**, 108.
Electricity, 123.
Elstead, 1, 5, 30, 48, 59, 64, 65, 68, 75, 78, 85, 94, 123.
Elvetham, 44, 47.
Emmett, 86.
Enclosure (Inclosure), 83, 93, 97, 101, 113.
Ewins, 114.
Falkner, 117.
Farnham,
    Battle of, **29**, 30.
    Castle, 32, 37, 39, 43, 63, 65.
    Corporation, 77-78.
    Hundred, 26, 31, **47**, 48, 67.
    Manor, 4, 7, 26, **27**, 28, 32-3, 35, 44, 49, 50, 51.
    Parish, 5, 62, 70, 107.
    Rural District Council, 5, 109, 114, 122, 126, 129.
St Andrew's Church, 27, 32, 56, 80.

Farnham (con):
   Town, 5, 32, 48, 62, 67, 80.
   Vestry, 77, 81, 84.
   Vicar of, 80, 84, 102.
   Wharf, 78.
   Workhouse, 80-1
Fire Service, **99**, 100
Fishing, 49, 80, 134.
Fitzwilliam, Sir William, 53, **53**.
Floyd 81, 117.
Football, 124-5.
Fox, John, 81,
Francklyn, 87.
French Occupation, 43-44.
Frensham, 1, 5, 28, 48, 58, 67, 68, 79, 132, 134.
Gas, 123.
Gibby, 127.
Godalming, 9, 62, 78, 97, 121.
Golf, 107, 125.
Green, Peter, 71-2
Greenstake, **45**.
Gregory, **63**.
Guildford, 9, 34, 40, 62, 69, 78.
Hambledon Rural District Council, 127, 129.
Hampden, Peter, 57, 58.
Hampton, 54.
Hankley Common, 107, 119, 129.
Hankley Common Golf Club, 107, 134.
Harding, 54, 59.
Harris, Absalom, 94.
Harris, Henry, 86, 91.
Hazell, 94, 127, 130.
Hearth Tax, 66-7, **67**.
Hitchcock, Richard, 59.
Holt, Rev Eardley, 86.
Hops, 69, 88, 105, 117.
Horse-riding & Hunting, 46, 70, 124, 134.
Hunter, Thomas Orby, 76.
Hurd-Wood, John, 117.
Ice Age, 12
Inwood, John, 59.

Ireton, Henry, 64.
Iron Age, 16, 17.
Islamabad, 133, **133**.
Jackson, Henry & Madge, 132.
Jay, Benedict, 54.
Johnson, Rev R.W., 86.
Jones, Rev W.T., 102.
Knight, 96, 114, 115.
Lagg, Alexander, 59.
Landscape, 8-10, 11, 17, 51, 76, 97, 118, 132.
Lay Subsidies, 48, 58, 68.
Lonsdale, 114, 117, 121.
Luff, William, 59.
Lussher, William 59.
Lutyens, Sir Edwin, 106, 108.
Lydger, John, 59.
Mangles, Frank, 95.
Mansell, 74, 81, 83, 93.
Marshall, 69-70, 95.
Matchwick, 74.
May, Thomas, 59.
Mayo-Perrott, Mrs, 131.
Mills, 12, 22, 33-4, 40, 41, 47, 48, 49, 77, 100, 129, 131.
Montague, Viscount, 54, 57.
Moody, Captain RN, 116.
Moon, 59, 60, **61**, 74, 81, 83.
Moor Park, 5, 67, 83, 84.
More, 54, 57.
National Trust, 12.
Nicholson, 86, 88, 93, 99, 106.
North, 131.
Novell, **55**, 59, 62.
Palmer, Robert, 44, 76.
Payne, William, 59.
Perry, 71.
Pierrepont, 79, 83, 84, 92, 98, 107, 131.
Pottery, 3, 8, 14, 20, **20**, 21, 22, 23, 24.
Poulter, Sam, 43.
Preston, Thomas, 59.
Price, Mr, 125.
Pyke, William, 54, 57.

Rabbit Warren, 46, 70.
Ragged School Shoe Black Society, 87.
Railway, 83, 90-1.
Reeves/Reves, 59, 62.
Rich, 76-7, 97, 132.
Roads, 90-1, **91**, 92, 97, 115-6.
Robo, Etienne, 38, 42, 50, 56.
Romans, 3, 7, 8, 18-23, 31.
Ross, Judith, 119.
Rushmoor, 1, 5-6, 97, 123.
Salt, Henry & Kate, **95**, 94-5.
Saxons, 24, 28, 32.
Seale, 5, 79, 86.
Shaw, George Bernard, 95, **95**.
Shotter, William, 77.
Shrobbe/Shrubb, 59, 81.
Skelton, 127.
Slea River, 21,
Smith, Charlotte, 87.
Smuggling, 78-80.
Stevens, Rev. Frederick, 86.
Stone Age, 11-14.
Stovold, 59, 60, 74, 75, 81, 83, 88, 93, 94, 127.
Strickland, Elizabeth, 94.
Sturt, George, 99, 118.
Surrey, 14, 18, 19, 24, 58, 62, 132.
Surrey County Council, 126, 132, 134.
Surrey Mission Society, 85, 105, 106.
Surrey Musters, 60.
Tayler, **73**, 73-4, **76**, 79, 80, 83, 84, 85, 86.
Tennis, 125.
Thomson, John, 83.
Til, 3
Tilbury, 111, **115**, 127.
Tilford:
    Bach Society, 126, 134.
    Bands, 105, **106**, 125, 126.
    Blacksmith. **ii**, 105.
    Bridges, 39-40, **40**, 46. 59. 78. 91. **92**, 114.
    Chapel, 72-3, **74**, **85**, 86, 105.
    Church, 12, 102-3, **102**, 108, 111, 133.

Tilford (cont):
    Clubs, 124-6, 134.
    Conservation Area, 134.
    Fete, 126.
    Garage, **115**, 133.
    Horticultural Society, 125, **125**, 134.
    Institute, 106-7, 111, 123, 126, 134.
    Maps, 2, **2**, 73, **75**.
    Mothers' Union, 107.
    Oaks, 30, 37, 105, **111**, 112-3, **112**, **113**, 114.
    Parish, 4-5, **4**
    Parish Council, 96-7, 109, **109**, 113, 127, 130, 134.
    Players, 126, 134.
    Police, 99-100.
    Population, 1, **6**, 6-7, 24, 34, 48, 60, 122.
    Post Office and shop, 111, **115**, 127, 133.
    Royal Visits, 116, 119-20.
    Schools, 21, **101**, 103-4, 114, 116-7, 120, 123, 127, 129, 132, 133.
    Sewers and Public Lavatory, 130-1.
    Sports, 107, 120, 124-5.
    War Memorial, 118, **120**, 121, 129.
    Wartime, 118-21, 128-9.
    Womens' Institute, 126, 134.
Tilford Bondlands:
    Bridgeland, 46, 56, **61**, 74, 78, 81, 83.
    Chapel Farm, 44, 46, 60, 73, 74.
    Coopers, 46, 74, 81.
    Earls, 46, 60, 75, 81, 83.
    Elthams, 48.
    Fishers, 74.
    Grovers, 46, 56, 83.
    Hatch, 56, 60.
    Hidemead, 74.
    Linches, **55**, 56, 75.
    Rede, 73.
    Sheephatch, 76, 83.
    Squires Hill Farm, 44, 74
    Stikkars, 46.
    Threshers, 74.
    Tilford, 46, 56, 73, 74.

Tilford Boundlands (cont):
  Tilford House Farm, 44, 73.
  Tilhill, 60, 75, 81, 83.
  Tuney, 56, 73.
  Widebrooks, 75.
  Widemead, 60, 75, 81, 83.
  Woodhill, 60, 74, 75, 83.
Tilford Farms:
  Chapel Farm, 86.
  Greenhills Farm, 95.
  Malthouse Farm, 130.
  Sheephatch Farm, 131.
  Squires Hill Farm, 93.
  Street Farm, 114, 127.
  Tilford House Farm, 91.
  Tilhill Farm, 64, 88.
  Upper Street Farm, 127.
  Woodhill Farm, 121, 127.
Tilford, Houses:
  Abbots Cottage, 121.
  Abbots Lodge, 94, 121.
  Abbots Pond Cottage, 121.
  Abbots Villa, (White Friars), 121.
  Archers Hill, 17, 121.
  Barrows, The, 16, 95, **96.**
  Brodge Cottage, 55.
  Bridge Farmhouse, 55, **63**.
  Chapel Farmhouse, **85**, 93.
  Charles Hill Court, 117.
  Chuter's Cottage, 58.
  Cobbett's Corner, 131.
  Crooksbury House, 96.
  Crooksbury Cottage, 131.
  Devona, 130.
  Eliot, 131.
  Gorse (South Bank Cottage), 94, **95**, 121.
  Greenhills, 95, 105, 121.
  Highmead, 117.
  Keepers Cottage, 132.
  Lane House, 121.
  Malthouse, 55, **61**.
  Monks Hill, 96, 114.
  Mount Pleasant Farm, 132.
  Normanswood, 96.

Tilford, Houses (cont):
  Oak (Beldams) Cottage, 105, **112**.
  Overwey, 20, 23, 117, 121.
  Quest, 122.
  Riversleigh, 95.
  Riversmeet, 127.
  Sheephatch Farmhouse, 55.
  Sheephatch House (Heathyfield), 102, 114, 119, 131.
  Squires Hill House, 96, 131.
  Stockbridge Cottages, 95, 100, 121.
  Street Farmhouse, 55.
  Tancreds Ford, 117.
  Tilford Cottage 86.
  Tile House, 121.
  Tilford Green Cottages, 55, 73.
  Tilford House, 71, **71**, 72-3, **74**, 84, **84**, 85, 88.
  Tilford House Farmhouse, 55.
  Tilhill House, 93, 132.
  Uplands, 117.
  Upper Street Farmhouse, 55, **55**.
  Waverley Cottage, 132.
  Waverley Hollow, 132.
  Well, 131.
  Wey Cottage, 93.
  Whitmead, 64, 96, 116, 117.
  Whitmead Sanatorium, 117.
  Yew Tree Cottage, 132.
Tilford Inns:
  Barley Mow, 73, 103, **104**, 105, **107**, **134**.
  Duke of Cambridge (Hankley), 94, 102, 107, 121, 134.
  Halfway House (Donkey), 94, 105.
Tilford Places:
  Abbots Plain, 93.
  Abbots Pond, 40, 46, 54, 59, 70, 94, 121.
  Birchen Reeds, 14, 44, 129.
  Black Lake, 40, 117.
  Botany Hill, 16.
  Boundstone Common, 93, 97.
  Camp Hill, 5.
  Chapel Field, 12.
  Charles Hill, 15, 16, 59, 83, 93-4, 96, 97.

Tilford Places (cont):
- Crooksbury, 14, 16, 37, 42, 54, 59, 63, 70, 76, 83, 93, 96, 97, 117, 131, 132.
- Grange Road, 97.
- Greenhills, 105, 132.
- Hankley Common, 13, 14, 108, 119, 130.
- Pierrepont Reeds, 54.
- Reeds, 8, 16, 59, 97, 123.
- Rural Life Centre (Old Kiln Museum), 54, 132.
- Sheephatch, 8, 16, 22, 39, 79, 91, 129.
- Shepherds Way, 127, 130.
- Smugglers' Way, 79.
- Squires Hill Lane, 127, 129.
- Stockbridge, 8, 13, 46, 73, 96, 134.
- Stonehills, 13, 101, 125.
- Street, The, 121, 123.
- Tancredsford/ Tankersford, 57, 79, 93, 132.
- Tilford Green, 37, 39, **110**.
- Tilford Meads, 123.
- Tilhill, 42.
- Wanford, 37-8, 44, 47, 73, 76.
- Whitemead, 8, 16, 20, 42, 73, 121, 130.
- Woodhill, 42.

Tilford House Estate, 72, 83, 84, 86, 121.
Tilford House Tenants, 74, 87.
Tilhill Estate, 127, 131.
Timson, William, 83.
Tithes, 87-8, **89**, 101.
Tithings, 5, 26, 48.
Tongham, 48, 50.
Troop Manoeuvres, 116, **116**.
Turner, 62, 71.
Ushabti, 22, **22**.
Vikings, 24, 28-9.
Waller, Sir William, 63, 64.

Ware:
- Anne, 83, 86, 87, 103, **103**.
- Charles, 86, 87, 97-8, 103.
- Edith, 119.
- Henry, 87.
- James, 87, **88**, 105, 106, 121.
- Joseph, 87.
- Margaret, 126.
- Martin, 83, 87, 93, 99.
- Martin Stewart, Rev, **88**, 114, 121, 122.
- Mary Violetta, **113**, 114.

Watson, Mrs, 117.
Waverley
- Abbey, 5, 33, 35-40, **36**, **38**, 43, 44, 57, 67, 131, 134.
- Abbey Dissolution, 52-3, 56.
- Abbey Estate, 76-7, 83, 86, 88, 127, 131.
- Abbey House, 62, 82, 84, 96, 118, 119, 131, 132.
- District (Borough) Council, 127, 130, 134.
- Valley, 9-10.

Weald, 8-9, 12.
West, John, 59.
Westbrook, William, 62, 75.
Wey, 1, 9, 12, 14, 17, 19, 21, 35, 43, 44, 49, 59, 78, 91, 114.
Wey Valley Water Co., 122-3.
Wheeler, Elizabeth, 104-5.
Whitehead, A.J., 131.
William the Conqueror, 32, 34, **35**.
Winchester,
- Bishop of, 28, 31, 32, 41, 46, 48, 51, 56, 77, 84, 86, 101, 113.
- City, 19, 21, 23, 32, 34, 38, 43.

Wood, Ralph, 79.